Research on
Religion and Aging

RESEARCH ON RELIGION AND AGING

An Annotated Bibliography

Compiled by

Harold G. Koenig

Bibliographies and Indexes in Gerontology, Number 27
Erdman B. Palmore, Series Adviser

GREENWOOD PRESS
Westport, Connecticut • London

Library of Congress Cataloging-in-Publication Data

Koenig, Harold George.
    Research on religion and aging : an annotated bibliography /
compiled by Harold G. Koenig.
        p. cm.—(Bibliographies and indexes in gerontology, ISSN
0743–7560 ; no. 27)
    Includes bibliographical references and indexes.
    ISBN 0–313–29427–5 (alk. paper)
    1. Aging—Religious aspects—Abstracts. 2. Aging—Religious
aspects—Indexes. 3. Aging—Religious aspects—Bibliography.
4. Aged—Pastoral counseling of—Abstracts. 5. Aged—Pastoral
counseling of—Indexes. 6. Aged—Pastoral counseling of—
Bibliography. I. Title. II. Series.
BL65.A46K64   1995
200′.84′6—dc20   94–44350

British Library Cataloguing in Publication Data is available.

Library of Congress Catalog Card Number: 94–44350
ISBN: 0–313–29427–5
ISSN: 0743–7560

First published in 1995

Greenwood Press, 88 Post Road West, Westport, CT 06881
An imprint of Greenwood Publishing Group, Inc.

Printed in the United States of America

The paper used in this book complies with the
Permanent Paper Standard issued by the National
Information Standards Organization (Z39.48–1984).

10 9 8 7 6 5 4 3 2 1

This book is dedicated to my supportive and loving wife, Charmin, my rambunctious six year old son, Jordan, and a precious little baby girl, Rebekah, who is on the way.

Contents

Series Foreword

The annotated bibliographies in this series provide answers to the fundamental question, "What is known?" Their purpose is simple, yet profound: to provide comprehensive reviews and references for the work done in various fields of gerontology. They are based on the fact that it is no longer possible for anyone to comprehend the vast body of research and writing in even one sub-specialty without years of work.

This fact has become true only in recent years. When I was an undergraduate (Class of '52) I think no one at Duke had even heard of gerontology. Almost no one in the world was identified as a gerontologist. Now there are over 6,000 professional members of the Gerontological Society of America. When I was an undergraduate, there were no courses in gerontology. Now there are thousands of courses offered by most major (and many minor) colleges and universities. When I was an undergraduate there was only one gerontological journal (the *Journal of Gerontology,* begun in 1945). Now there are over forty professional journals and several dozen books in gerontology published each year.

The reasons for this dramatic growth are well known: the dramatic increase in numbers of aged, the shift from family to public responsibility for the security and care of the elderly, the recognition of aging as a "social problem," and the growth of science in general. It is less well known that this explosive growth in knowledge has developed the need for new solutions to the old problem of comprehending, and "keeping up" with a field of knowledge. The old indexes and library card catalogues have become increasingly inadequate for the job. On-line computer indexes and abstracts are one solution but make no evaluative selections nor organize sources logically as is done here. These annotated bibliographies are also more widely available than on-line computer indexes.

These bibliographies will obviously be useful for students, teachers, and researchers who need to know what research has (or has not) been done in their field. This particular bibliography will also be useful to sociologists of religion, ministers, mental health workers, geriatricians, nurses, and clinical social workers. The annotations contain enough information so that the user usually does not have to search out the original articles.

In the past, the "review of literature" has often been haphazard and was rarely comprehensive, because of the large investment of time (and money) that would be required by a truly comprehensive review. Now, using these bibliographies, researchers and others concerned with this topic can be more confident that they are not missing important previous research and other reports; they can be more confident that they are not duplicating past efforts and "reinventing the wheel". It may well become standard and expected practice for researchers to consult such bibliographies, even before they start their research.

The research relevant to religion and aging has become a large and rapidly growing field, especially in the last decade. This is attested to by the nearly 300 references since 1980 in this bibliography, and by the wide variety of disciplines represented here. Thus this volume will be useful to teachers, other professionals, and researchers in many different fields.

The author has done an outstanding job of covering the recent literature and organizing it into easily accessible form. Not only are the entries organized into four parts, ten sections, and numerous sub-sections, but there is an introduction, a sub-section on modeling religion's effects, and the author's conclusions from a synthesis of the literature on spirituality and health. There are also comprehensive subject and author indexes.

Thus one can look for relevant material in this volume in several ways: (1) look up a given subject in the subject index; (2) look up a given author in the author index; or (3) turn to the section and sub-section that covers the subject in which you are interested.

Harold Koenig is exceptionally well-qualified to produce this bibliography. He has long been a specialist in this area, has done significant research, has published several articles and books on religion and aging, and recently has announced a new program, which he directs, on "Religion, Aging, and Health" at the Duke Center for the Study of Aging.

So it is with great pleasure that we add this bibliography to our series. We believe you will find this volume to be the most useful, comprehensive, and easily accessible reference work in its field. I will appreciate any comments you care to send me.

Erdman B. Palmore
Center for the Study of Aging and Human Development
Box 3003, Duke University Medical Center
Durham, NC 27710

Introduction

Research on Religion and Aging is an annotated bibliography that catalogues and reviews recently published research between 1980 and 1995. This volume builds on the previous reviews of Paul Maves (1960), Thomas Cook (1976), and Vincent Fecher (1982) who provide detailed bibliographies of studies done between 1950 and 1980 (including the early work of David Moberg and the Catholic Digest surveys). Professionals involved in research, education, public health, health care policy, and a wide variety of clinical disciplines related to aging or religion will find this bibliography useful -- social geronto-logists, sociologists of religion, all mental health professionals, geriatricians, nurses, and clinical social workers. Policy-analysts will find here a ready resource for identifying the most rigorous and methodologically sound research in the field.

The topic of religion and its effects on health is receiving increased attention by researchers, educators, and policy makers in the aging field, not only because of its wide prevalence, but because of its potential as a resource to help meet the projected health needs of our aging population over the next 40 years. In the year 2025, nearly one-third of the U.S. population will be age 55 or over (U.S. Senate Committee, 1988). Improved medical care is enabling persons to live longer, but with disability and chronic health problems (Kunkel & Applebaum, 1992). This, along with high rates of depression, anxiety, and substance abuse among aging baby boomers (Weissman & Klerman, 1989), has caused some to predict a near epidemic of mental health problems among older adults in the first half of the 21st century (Koenig, et al., 1994). Given the already overwhelming federal deficit (4 trillion dollars) and evolving plans to limit increases in Medicare expenditures, it is not clear where the funding will come from for geriatric health care (particularly mental health care) in the year 2020.

Health promotion and disease prevention are now receiving more attention, and alternative resources within the community are being scrutinized to possibly supplement state and federal programs. Prior to state and federal programs for the sick, mentally ill, or aged, religious institutions commonly cared for these individuals; they may once again have an opportunity to do so. Thus, it is of utmost importance to better understand the effects of religious beliefs and behaviors on health, and how these change with aging. Within the past 15 years, a number of research studies have specifically addressed such questions using contemporary research methods.

In each section of this volume, including the subsections, annotations are grouped primarily by subject content and secondarily by date of publication and specific author. The first section (Part I) focuses on studies that explore patterns of religious belief, attitude, experience, private and public practice among older adults, and examine how these factors change with aging; included here is a section on religious faith development in later life. The second section (Part II) includes studies that address the relationship between religion and health (physical and psychological), including disease prevention. Part II receives the greatest attention because of its clinical and public policy relevance, and because of the author's special interest and background in geriatric medicine, psychiatry, and nursing.

The third section (Part III) reviews studies which bring together and interpret research findings to make recommendations for those who work with the elderly; a number of theoretical and review papers are presented in this section. Part IV presents papers on the measurement of religiosity, spirituality, and similar constructs; included here are studies that assess the reliability and validity of commonly used instruments. Finally, the Conclusion provides a summary and brief synthesis of the research on religion and aging. Included here is a description of a comprehensive explanatory model that depicts how religious factors influence a person's mental health through many different avenues, both in the present and during one's lifetime. The first model (Figure 1) describes how religion might prevent the onset of emotional disorder in later life; a second model (Figure 2) outlines how religion might help to resolve emotional disorder should it develop.

While the research on religion and aging has been briefly addressed in a number of publications (Lefevre & Lefevre, 1981; Clements, 1983; Clements, 1988; Koenig, et al., 1988; Levin, 1988; Clements, 1989; Koenig, 1990; Seeber, 1990; Simmons & Pierce, 1992; Sherrill, et al., 1993; Levin, 1993; Koenig, 1994; Thomas & Eisenhandler, 1994; Kimble, et al., 1995; McFadden, 1995), there is no central source to which educators, policy makers, or researchers can turn that comprehensively, succinctly, and systematically summarizes the *latest* research in the field -- particularly that pertaining to mental and physical health. Because of the rapid growth in the sophistication of research methodology and, consequently, the increased quality of work being published, it is essential that such a source identifying new studies be available -- including a comment on their merit. While I include a number of secondary articles and books that bring together and interpret the research findings for practical application, the distinguishing characteristic of this bibliography is its focus on the original research -- the nature of the samples, the types of instruments used, the statistical methods, the size of effects, and the overall quality of data collected and conclusions derived.

The procedure used to identify studies for inclusion in this bibliography is as follows. The medical, nursing, psychology, and sociology literature was reviewed from 1980 to 1995 using PsycLIT, MEDLINE, and Sociofile computer databases. In addition, major medical, psychiatric, and sociological journals were scanned between 1980 and 1995 for published research on religion and aging. Finally, major textbooks were reviewed for studies that provided important contributions to the field. Almost 300 articles in all are cited and summarized. Comments are subdivided into five categories: study *objective, sample and methods, results, conclusions*, and a comment on *quality* (fair, good, very good, excellent). This structure should allow the reader to quickly evaluate and easily access the most recent works in the field, facilitating the identification of individual papers and works by specific authors.

Most studies reported here have found a positive relationship between religious beliefs, behaviors, and mental or physical health; this is despite a most ardent search by the author for research demonstrating otherwise. It is likely that "neutral" studies, e.g., those that fail to show an association, seldom get published. This bias, however, is true for published research on relations between any psychosocial variable and health. Journal editors know that the absence of an association is of less interest to readers than either a negative or a positive effect, and consequently seldom publish the former unless the methodology is of the highest quality. This makes sense; poorly designed studies are often unable to detect a true effect (Type II error) since their methodology introduces excess variability to the data. On the other hand, systematic bias can also create the finding of an association that does not really exist. Because of the strong opinions by many that religion either has a positive or a negative effect on the health of older adults, it is necessary to be vigilant for such bias in the methodology in the studies reviewed. Nevertheless, one would expect such a bias to work both ways. The dearth of published studies showing a *negative* relationship between religion and health (particularly mental health) in older adults, then, says as much as the abundant reports documenting a positive association.

It is also important to remember that the relationship between aging, religion, and health is a dynamic one -- aging and health impacting on religious behaviors, and vice-versa. Cross-sectional studies, which make up the vast majority of published reports to date, are but a snapshot of the relationship, and tell little about this constantly changing, vibrant interaction. Thus, special attention will be paid to the few longitudinal studies on this topic and to their contributions to the knowledge base gathered largely from cross-sectional work.

Finally, this bibliography focuses primarily on studies that involve older adults. I have taken the liberty, however, to cover certain works that either include persons of all ages or, more rarely, only younger subjects. I have done this when the studies in younger adults have special relevance for the elderly and there exists little or no research in older subjects that addresses the topic.

References

Clements, W.M. 1983. Ministry with the Aging: Design, Challenges, Foundations. San Francisco: Harper & Row.

Clements, W.M. 1988. Religion, Aging and Health: A Global Perspective. NY: Haworth Press.

Clements, W.M. 1989. Ministry with the Aging: Designs, Challenges, Foundations. New York: Haworth Press.

Cook, T.C. 1976. The Religious Sector Explores its Mission in Aging. Athens, GA: National Interfaith Coalition on Aging.

Fecher, V.J. 1982. Religion & Aging: Annotated Bibliography. San Antonio, TX: Trinity University Press.

Kimble, M., S. McFadden, J. Ellor, and J. Seeber. 1995. Aging, Religion and Spirituality: A Handbook. Minneapolis, MN: Fortress Press.

Klerman, G.L., and M.M. Weissman. 1989. Increasing rates of depression. Journal of the American Medical Association 261:2229-2235.

Koenig, H.G., M. Smiley, and A.P. Gonzales. 1988. Religion, Health and Aging. Westport, CT: Greenwood Press.

Koenig, H.G. 1990. Research on religion and mental health in later life: a review and commentary. Journal of Geriatric Psychiatry 23(1):23-53.

Koenig, H.G. 1994. Aging and God. New York: Haworth Press.

Koenig, H.G., L.K. George, and R. Schneider. 1994. Mental health care for older adults in the year 2020: A dangerous and avoided topic. The Gerontologist 34:674-679.

Kunkel, S.R., and R.A. Applebaum. 1992. Estimating the prevalence of long-term disability for an aging society. Journal of Gerontology 47:S253-S260.

Lefevre, C., and P. Lefevre. 1981. Aging and the Human Spirit: A Reader in Religion and Gerontology. Chicago: Exploration Press.

Levin, J.S. 1988. Religious factors in aging, adjustment and health: a theoretical overview. Journal of Religion and Aging 4:133-145.

Levin, J.S. 1993. Religion in Aging and Health. Thousand Oaks, CA: Sage Publications.

Maves, P.B. 1960. Aging, religion, and the Church. In C. Tibbitts (Ed.), Handbook of Social Gerontology. Chicago: University of Chicago Press, pp. 698-748.

McFadden, S. 1995. In J.E. Birren, K.W. Schaie (eds), Handbook of the Psychology of Aging (4th ed). San Diego: Academic Press.

MEDLINE. 1989-94. National Library of Congress, Washington, DC. SilverPlatter Software 3.11, Silver Platter International, copyright 1992.

PsycLIT Database. 1994. Copyright 1990-94 by American Psychological Association (Silver Platter 3.11).

Seeber, J.J. 1990. Spiritual Maturity in the Later Years. New York: Haworth Press.

xviii   Research on Religion and Aging

Sherrill, K.A., D.B. Larson, and M. Greenwold. 1993. Is religion taboo in geriatrics?: Systematic review of research on religion in three major gerontologic journals, 1985-1991. American Journal of Geriatric Psychiatry 1:109-117.

Simmons, H.C., and V.S. Pierce. 1992. Pastoral Responses to Older Adults and Their Families: An Annotated Bibliography. Westport, CT: Greenwood Press.

Sociofile Database. 1974-1994. Sociological abstracts and SOPODA. University Microfilms International (SilverPlatter 3.11).

Thomas, L.E. and S.A. Eisenhandler. 1994. Aging and the Religious Dimension. Westport, CT: Auburn House.

U.S. Special Committee on Aging. 1988. Aging America - Trends and Projections. Washington, DC, U.S. Department of Health and Human Services, 1987-1988, p 11.

Part I

Religious Beliefs, Behaviors, and Experience

BELIEFS, ATTITUDES, AND COMMITMENT

Community-Dwelling Elderly

1. Glamser, F.D. 1987. The impact of retirement on religiosity. Journal of Religion and Aging 4(1):27-37.
Objective: Examines mean levels of belief and church attendance during years before and after retirement. *Sample & Methods*: Longitudinal panel study of 51 Pennsylvania industrial workers over six years. Subjects were all 60 years or over at the start of the study (mean 62 years), came from small towns and were socially conservative; three quarters were Protestant and one-quarter Catholic. Work was mostly assembly line and semi-skilled; mean education was 10 years. Subjects were interviewed once pre-retirement and once post-retirement (average 3.7 years). Single items measuring church attendance (range 1-5) and belief in God (range 1-6) were asked at both surveys, and a question about changing importance of religion only in the second survey. *Results*: Mean church attendance and belief in God were roughly the same on both surveys; however, for church attendance, there was a movement toward extremes - either once/wk or rarely if at all - with the middle categories dropping out. Belief in God, on the other hand, did not change. The relationship between belief and church attendance increased post-retirement ($r = .11$ to $r = .29$). When asked if religion had changed since retirement, 37% reported more important and 59% reported no change; only one person said it was less important. *Conclusions*: There appears to be more individual change in religious belief and behavior in late adulthood than

previously thought. *Quality*: Good. Weak measures of religiosity to assess change; results are consistent with the work of others in community (Courtenay et al. 1992, below) and clinical settings (Koenig 1994, Ch 9, below).

2. Sasaki, M. 1987. Changes in religious commitment in the United States, Holland, and Japan. American Journal of Sociology 92:1055-1076.

Objective: Using Bayesian cohort analysis, the author examines changes in religious commitment over age, historical period, and generation in three countries. *Sample & Methods*: For the United States, the investigator used survey data from the Institute of Social Research at University of Michigan gathered every two years from 1952 to 1982. Religious commitment was measured by regular or weekly church attendance. For Holland, data from national surveys by the Central Bureau of Statistics between 1899 and 1969 were used. Again, religious affiliation or non-affiliation was the only indicator of commitment. For the Japanese, data were used from National Character Surveys conducted at 5-year intervals by the Institute of Statistical Mathematics between 1953 and 1983. Because temple or shrine attendance is not relevant in this culture, religious belief was the indicator of religious commitment (Do you have any religious faith?). *Results*: For the United States, church attendance remained stable over the 30 years; however, the percentage of frequent church attenders increased steadily after age 45 into old age. Analysis revealed cohort effects, such that church attendance began dropping for generations born after 1927 (partially supporting the secularization hypothesis during recent generations). The data from Holland showed an increasing likelihood from 1899 to 1969 of religious non-affiliation (1.8% to 23.0%). A weak age effects was also seen; the percentage of those with a religious affiliation increased steadily beyond age 30 into old age (as in the U.S.). Religious non-affiliation was particularly common among those born after 1940, supporting the secularization hypothesis. Religious belief in Japan was relatively stable between 1953 and 1983. Strong age effects, however, were present; "the aging process tends to influence the Japanese people to become progressively more religious, with the younger japanese being potential religious believers" (p 1069) (not providing support for the secularization hypothesis). *Conclusions*: Secularization cannot be viewed as a global phenomenon, but rather as due to generational difference factors and domestic sociohistorical events. In Japan, in particular, the aging process itself has a significant effect on religious belief. *Quality*: Very good.

3. Courtenay, B.C., L.W. Poon, P. Martin, G.M. Clayton, and M.A. Johnson. 1992. Religiosity and adaptation in the oldest-old. International Journal of Aging and Human Development 34(1): 47-56.

Objective: Examines the relationship between religiosity, age, and health in a sample that includes centenarians. *Sample & Methods*: Cross-sectional sample of 165 persons ages 60 to 100+ years participating in the Georgia Centenarian Study. Coping was measured using the Health and Daily Living Scale and religiosity was measured using an instrument developed by Faulkner and DeJong. *Results:* There was a trend towards increasing religiosity with age (p = .069). A close inspection of the outcomes of the multivariate analysis demonstrated that three of the five religiosity dimensions increased significantly with age: ideological (F = 4.9, p < .01), intellectual (f = 4.9, p < .01), and consequential (F = 3.1, p < .05). Furthermore, overall religiosity and each of the five dimensions of religiosity had their highest average scores among the Centenarians (n = 31). Religiosity was also correlated with neurological and musculoskeletal problems; furthermore, individuals with more severe health problems were more likely to indicate higher participation levels in the ritualistic dimension of religiosity. Religiosity was unrelated to mental health. *Conclusions*: The data suggest that there may be a linear increase in religiosity with age, especially for beliefs, knowledge about religion, and reliance on religion in daily life. Religiosity and poorer physical health were significantly related, although there was no relationship with mental health or life satisfaction. Religious coping may be more important in the oldest-old than in younger adults or in younger elderly. *Quality*: Very Good.

4. Degenova, M.K. 1992. If you had your life to live over again: What would you do differently? International Journal of Aging and Human Development 34:135-143.

Objective: Examines how older persons would change the amount of time spent on various activities during adulthood. *Results*: 54% of elders said that they would not change the amount of time devoted to religion; however, over one-third (35%) reported that they wished they had spent more time on religion. Less than 2% indicated a wish to have spent less time on religion. *Conclusions*: A significant proportion of older adults regret that they did not direct more time during their adult years to religious matters. *Quality*: Good.

5. Isenberg, S. 1992. Aging in Judaism: "Crown of glory" and "days of sorrow." In T.R. Cole, D.D. Van Tassel, R. Kastenbaum (eds), Handbook of the Humanities and Aging.

New York: Springer, pp 147-174.
Objective: Surveys Jewish literature to obtain a sense of what
"growing old" means in this religion. *Sample & Methods*: Literature
review and discussion. *Results & Conclusions*: Most of the early
Jewish scriptures focus primarily on aging as viewed by males in
society; only in recent times has the woman's view of aging been
expressed, indicating that it may be quite different from that of Jewish
men. *Quality*: Good. Also see Kart, C.S. 1987. Age and religious
commitment in the American-Jewish community. In Gelfand, D.E.,
Barresi, C.M. (Eds.), Ethnic Dimensions of Aging. NY: Springer, pp
96-105.

6. Jernigan, H.L., and M.B. Jernigan. 1992. Aging in a Chinese
   society. Journal of Religious Gerontology 8(3):1-111 (entire
   issue).
Objective: Senior authors spent time in Taiwan and Singapore studying
the social, psychological, and religious aspects of aging in these
cultures. *Sample & Methods*: Unstructured interviews with a purposive
sample of older adults living in Taiwan and Singapore. *Results and
Conclusions*: Of particular interest from a mental health perspective,
is their report of invaluable information on how elders used (or did not
use) their Confucian and Buddhist religions to help them to cope with
or transcend adversity and day to day hardships (especially pp. 73-93).
Quality: Good. One of the few unbiased sources of information about
the relationship between Confucianism, Buddhism, and mental health
of aging Chinese.

7. Thursby, G.R. 1992. Islamic, Hindu, and Buddhist conceptions
   of aging. In T.R. Cole, D.D. Van Tassel, R. Kastenbaum (eds),
   Handbook of the Humanities and Aging. New York: Springer,
   pp 175-196.
Objective: Examines how aging is viewed in three world religions
whose members make up nearly 40% of the earth's population.
Sample & Methods: Discussion. *Results & Conclusions*: There are both
common themes and differences that distinguish how each religious
tradition views the aging process and provides it with meaning. All
three traditions assume that life is precious and can be understood only
in terms of transcendent reality. Islam discourages ascetic life styles
and emphasizes the family; according the Quaran, aging is a sign of
Allah's mercy, justice, and power. In contrast, Buddhism centers on
the monastic life; focusing on the renunciation of this life, it draws
peoples' attentions to the suffering that occurs in old age to motivate
them towards detachment from this world; there is an emphasis on
calming of the self and on sensing the "ageless presence". Hinduism,

on the other hand, tries to balance the priorities of monasticism and family life; manifesting itself in diverse traditions and rituals, Hinduism views the life cycle as being constantly renewed in order to achieve movement into the upper three Indian castes. *Quality*: Good.

Clinical Populations

8. Koenig, H.G., D.O. Moberg, and J.N. Kvale. 1988. Religious activities and attitudes of older adults in a geriatric assessment clinic. Journal of the American Geriatrics Society 36:362-374.
Objective: Assesses the prevalence of orthodox Christian religious beliefs, behaviors, and intrinsic religious attitudes among older persons attending a geriatric medicine clinic, and relates these religious variables with health factors such as hypertension, smoking, cancer, dementia, and so forth. *Sample & Methods*: 106 consecutive elderly patients (mean age 74.4 years) attending a family medicine geriatric clinic in Springfield, Illinois, completed the long-version of the Springfield Religiosity Schedule; medical conditions were assessed by physical examination and chart review. *Results*: A high prevalence of orthodox Christian beliefs, activities, and intrinsic religious attitudes were reported. Religious activities and attitudes were lower among patients with cancer, chronic anxiety, depression, and those who smoked cigarettes or consumed moderate to large amounts of alcohol; intrinsic religious attitudes were also less common among men with hypertension. *Conclusion*: These results suggest that religion is a powerful cultural force in the lives of older medical patients and is integrally related to both mental and physical health. This is among the most detailed report of its kind on religious beliefs and behaviors in geriatric medical patients.

9. Bearon, L.B., and H.G. Koenig. 1990. Religious cognitions and use of prayer in health and illness. The Gerontologist 30:249-253.
Objective: Explores older adults' beliefs about God's role in health and illness and about their use of prayer in response to specific physical symptoms. *Sample & Methods*: Face to face structured interviews with 40 community-dwelling adult volunteers aged 65 to 74 years; sample consisted of 50% men and 50% women, 48% White and 52% Black, median education of 12 years, 48% Baptist and 25% Methodists, and 65% self-rated health of good or excellent. *Results*: Three-quarters (74%) disagreed with statements indicating that sickness was a test by God to determine a person's strength of faith or that physical illness comes from God as a punishment for sin. Respondents averaged three

physical symptoms each; 53% reported praying about at least one
symptoms the last time they experienced it.   Use of prayer was
associated with lower education, Baptist denomination, and Blacks.
Symptoms discussed with a physician or for which drugs were taken,
were more likely to be prayed about.   *Conclusions*:   Health
professionals will be able to elicit more complete information on their
client's cognitive models of health and illness by asking specific
questions about religious beliefs.

10. Koenig, H.G., M. Hover, L.B. Bearon, and J.L. Travis. 1991.
     Religious perspectives of doctors, nurses, patients, and
     families: Some interesting differences. Journal of Pastoral Care
     45:254-267.

Objective: Explores differences in the religious beliefs and practices of
health professionals and the patients they serve. *Sample & Methods*:
Questionnaires were completed by 130 physicians (12% response
rate), 39 nurses (42% response), 77 patients (38% response), and
patients' families (92% response) at Duke University Medical Center.
Thirty-six percent of patients were over age 60. *Results*: Physicians
were less likely than other groups to believe in a "Higher Power,"
attend church weekly, and use religious beliefs to cope; 18% of
physician were of the Jewish faith or were agnostic (9%), whereas 0%
of the other three groups were. Psychiatrists were the least religious
and made the fewest referrals to chaplains. *Conclusions*: The religious
beliefs and practices of physicians in this study contrasted with those
of their patients.   Given these differences, it is uncertain whether
physician's are able to comprehend and address the spiritual needs of
physically ill hospitalized patients (many of whom are elderly and highly
religious).

11. Koenig, H.G. 1995. Religion and older men in prison.   Inter-
     national Journal of Geriatric Psychiatry, in press.

Objective: Examines the religious characteristics and background of
federal inmates age 50 or over, and the relationship to psychological
adjustment to prison life.   *Sample & Methods*: The sample was
composed of 96 of 106 (91% response rate) older male inmates at a
Federal Correctional Institution in Butner, North Carolina. Participants
in the study, ages 50 to 72 years, came from all over the United States
to be incarcerated at this minimum to high security risk prison; the
average length of sentence was 8 years, and this was the first prison
term for 49% of the sample.   An extensive list of religious
characteristics was measured. *Results*: 80% of inmates had switched
out of the denomination in which they were raised, with a net
movement away from conservative Protestant toward mainline

Protestant traditions. Religious inmates were more likely to be serving their first prison term and had fewer disciplinary actions levied against them.   For 32% of inmates, religion was reported to be the most important factor than enabled them to cope. Intrinsic religiosity and perceived importance of religion to their parents were both inversely related to depressive symptoms. *Conclusions*: Religious beliefs, activities, experience, and internal motivations toward religion are common among older inmates, and these factors are important for psychological adjustment to prison. This is the first and only study of religious characteristics of older federal prisoners.

Religious and Spiritual Development

12. Hall, E.G. 1985. Spirituality during aging. Pastoral Psychology 34(2):112-117.
Objective: Examines the process of spiritual maturation in the context of developmental models of aging. *Sample & Methods*: Case study of 3 elderly nursing home residents. *Results & Conclusions*: Carl Jung's perspectives on the psychodynamics of the human spirit is compared with Gordon Allport's description of mature religiosity. *Quality*: Fair

13. Pruyser, P.W. 1987. Where do we go from here? Scenarios for the psychology of religion. Journal for the Scientific Study of Religion 26:173-181.
Objective: Dr. Pruyser (professor emeritus of psychology at the Menninger Foundation) discusses basic elements for a comprehensive psychology of religion, and makes recommendations for needed new studies and approaches. *Sample & Methods*: Discussion. No data are presented. Only 7 references (two by the primary author). *Results & Conclusions*: The conclusion relevant to research on religion and aging from this paper is Dr. Pruyser's recommendation that "Leaning on a classical reflection about projection made by Feuerbach and Freud and many others, I would like to see studies done on aspects of religious experience and attitudes in aging people and old folks." He predicts that ". . . if personality development implies emancipation from childhood needs and an increasing awareness of one's own projections, one would expect that some people's notions of deity will shed their anthropomorphic features and will be replaced entirely by a more abstract principle of cosmic creativity, ethical value, or ultimate truth . . . Their religiousness may become atheistic in the sense that they no longer feel impelled to pay homage to a quasi-human God in worship and prayer . . . Moreover, from introspective self-study I must affirm that something like this process has slowly and steadily been

happening to me..." *Quality*: Fair. There is <u>no evidence</u> from the hundreds of scientific studies presented in *Research on Religion and Aging* that people "outgrow" their traditional religious beliefs as they become older; if anything, these beliefs become stronger and more useful for coping.

14.   Shulik, R.N. 1988. Faith development in older adults.   Special
      Issue: Religion and aging.   <u>Educational Gerontology</u> 14:291-
      301.
Objective: Assesses the generalizability of James Fowler's theory of faith development to older adults. *Sample & Methods*: Convenience sample of 20 elderly men and 20 elderly women, none of whom had chronic illness.   Because the small sample size limits statistical comparison, findings are reported in a subjective rather than objective manner. *Results*: Subjects in the intermediate stages of faith (not the higher stages) demonstrated the lowest level of depression, and thus, the best adaptation. There was a relationship between increasing intelligence and increasing faith development. *Conclusion*: Fowler's faith development paradigm can make a meaningful contribution to gerontology.   *Quality*: Fair; less than a powerful demonstration of support for Fowler's theory in older adults. [For Fowler's theory, see Fowler, J.   1981.   <u>Stages of Faith</u>.   San Francisco: Harper & Row Publishers.]

15.   Worthington, E.L.   1989. Religious faith across the life-span:
      Implications for counseling and research.   <u>The Counseling
      Psychologist</u> 17:555-612.
Objective: Examines religious development from childhood through late adulthood, reviewing the theories and the research that backs them up. *Sample & Methods*: Literature review and discussion. *Results*: First, theories of psychological and religious development are reviewed (Piaget, Elkind, Kohlberg, Erikson, Alport, Fowler); emphasis is placed on "life event" or "transition theory" perspectives, particularly for religious development from adolescence and thereafter.   Second, research on this topic is reviewed. Third, implications for theory and research are discussed, and important questions are identified that need to be answered. *Conclusions*: Psychologists can benefit in the areas of assessment, counseling, and research by understanding the religious development of their clients across the lifespan. *Quality*: Very good.   A comprehensive and well-written review of the topic from a psychologist's perspective.

16.   Jecker, N.S. 1990.   Adult moral development: Ancient,
      medieval, & modern paths. <u>Generations</u> (Fall issue):19-24.

Objective: Focuses on different historical approaches to adult moral development, tracing their origins in ancient Greece through the Middle Ages to modern times. *Sample & Methods*: Historical review and discussion. *Results & Conclusions*: Examines the attitudes of Plato, Aristotle, Augustine, and Kohlberg, comparing and contrasting their theories of moral development. *Quality*: Fair. Spiritual development appears only peripheral to the main topic.

17. McFadden, S., and R.R. Gerl. 1990. Approaches to understanding spirituality in the second half of life. Generations 14(4):35-38.
Objective: Examines psychological models of development that may be applied to faith development in later life. *Sample & Methods*: Literature review and discussion. *Results & Conclusions*: The life-span model of human development can be used to integrate psychological, physical, social, and spiritual changes that occur with aging. *Quality*: Good.

18.   Oser, F.K. 1991.   Religious Judgement: A Developmental Approach. Birmingham, AL: Religious Education Press
Objective: Examines the relationship between religious development and cognitive development. *Results & Conclusions*: Cognitive development may drive religious development, with maturity in religious judgements coming about through choices made in response to religious dilemmas. *Quality*: Good.   For more reading on the relationship between cognitive and religious development see: Sinnott, J.D. 1994. Development and learning: Cognitive aspects of spiritual development.   Journal of Adult Development 1:91-99 [Explores whether persons actively engaged in spiritual matters are actually operating at a "postformal" level of thought]; Koplowitz, H. 1990. Unitary consciousness and the highest development of mind: The relation between spiritual development and cognitive development. In M.L. Commons, C. Armon, L. Kohlberg, F.A. Richards, T.A. Grotzer, J.D. Sinnott (eds), Adult Development (vol 2): Models and Methods in the Study of Adolescent and Adult Thought. NY: Praeger, pp 105-111. [Argues that spiritual development is noncognitive and thus should not be linked with postformal cognitive styles.]

19.   Pratt, M.W., B. Hunsberger, M.S. Pencer, and D. Roth. 1992. Reflections   on   religion: Aging,   belief   orthodoxy,   and interpersonal conflict in the complexity of adult thinking about religious issues.   Journal for the Scientific Study of Religion 31:514-522.
Objective: Explores the complexity and degree of integration of reasoning by persons in three age groups about three types of religious issues. *Sample & Methods*: The three age groups were 18-26 years

(n = 21), 27-45 years (n = 22), and 60-86 (n = 17). The three religious issues were: (1) a personal conflict religious issue (of the subjects' own report), (2) a personal nonconflict issue, and (3) the evolutionist vs. creationist account of human origins. *Results*: The complexity of reasoning of older adults about these issues was lower than that of the younger age groups. Subjects who were older and had more orthodox beliefs displayed less religious reflection, poorer verbal skills, and overall less integration and complexity of religious thought. *Quality*: Good. A most interesting study. Of course, "complexity of religious thought" may not be the standard to strive after. Indeed, traditional Judeo-Christian doctrine holds that it is the most simple faith - the faith held by a child - that is the key which unlocks the power of religious faith. In my opinion, the authors make the same mistake as Shulik (ref 13 above) in associating religious or faith development with intelligence or cognitive complexity.

20.   Reich, K.H. 1993.   Cognitive developmental approaches to religiousness: Which version for which purpose. International Journal for the Psychology of Religion 3:145-171.
Objective: Examines religious development during the adult years. *Sample & Methods*: Literature review and discussion. *Results & Conclusions*: Research on religious development during adulthood (primarily in non-clinical samples) indicates a pattern of stability and lack of change. *Quality*: Fair. Because of the link between religious development and psychosocial stress, these results may not apply to clinical samples or to older adults experiencing negative events and adverse life circumstances.

21. Koenig, H.G. 1994. Theories of human development (Ch 5). In H.G. Koenig, Aging and God. NY: Haworth Press, pp. 67-85.
Objective: Examines each of the major theories of human development with a special focus on development in later life. Provides a brief review of major theories of human development relevant to older adults. *Sample & Methods*: Literature review and discussion. *Results*: Gergen's division of developmental theories into three types provides the underlying structure for this chapter. The types include the stability account (Freud), the ordered change account (Erikson, Piaget, Kohlberg, Buhler), and the aleatoric account (Jung, Sullivan, Maslow, Allport). *Conclusion*: The aleatoric account is most consistent with recent clinical experience and easily harmonizes with a religious world-view. This account sees humans as active rather than reactive in their responses to environmental events. Growth is determined by decisions and choices that persons make.

22. Koenig, H.G. 1994. Fowler's stages of faith development (Ch 6). In H.G. Koenig, Aging and God. NY: Haworth Press, pp. 87-104.
Objective: Reviews and critiques Fowler's theory of faith development. *Sample & Methods*: Literature review and discussion. *Results & Conclusions*: Fowler's theory as having serious flaws when attempting to generalize it to older adults. Few older adults were included in the original sample upon which the theory was tested. Relies heavily on educational level and cognitive development, and may not be applicable to lower socioeconomic groups or chronically ill elderly with cognitive impairments. Shulik's work (above) is also reviewed and critiqued (ref #14).

23. Koenig, H.G. 1994. A theory of religious faith development (Ch 7). In H.G. Koenig, Aging and God. NY: Haworth Press, pp 105-135.
Objective: Seeks to develop a theory of religious faith development that is applicable to adults of all ages, especially older adults. *Sample & Methods*: Literature review and discussion. Uses data from several sources (epidemiological studies and religious texts) to support theory. *Results & Conclusions*: Defines religious faith in terms of relationship with God. Mature faith is seen as a solid, unwavering belief and trust in God as one's ultimate source; this enables the older person to weather changes in their physical, emotional, and social environments, develop and maintain satisfying interpersonal relationships, and achieve a sense of purpose and meaning in later life. This theory, unlike Fowler's, does not attempt to be all inclusive; rather, it focuses on faith development specifically in the Judeo-Christian faith community (in which over 90% of older Americans belong).

24. Koenig, H.G. 1994. Religion as cognitive schema: Comments on H. McIntosh. International Journal of the Psychology of Religion 5(1) (in press)
Objective: Comments on H. McIntosh's article that conceptualizes religion as a cognitive schema. *Sample & Methods*: Literature review and discussion. *Results & Conclusions*: The concept of religious cognitive schema is useful for understanding how persons use religion to help cope with stress of physical illness, and for understanding the impact of physical illness on religious faith. Nevertheless, there are limitations to conceptualizing religion as cognitive schema, particularly with regard to measurement. Clinical implications of religious cognitive schema are also discussed for mental health professionals and those doing therapy with religious patients.

25.   Payne, B. 1994.   Faith development in older men.   In E.H.
       Thompson (ed), <u>Older Men's Lives</u>. Newbury Park, CA: Sage
       Publications.
Objective: Examines James Fowler's theory of faith development as it
might apply to older men. *Sample & Methods*: Literature review and
discussion. *Results & Conclusions*: No major gender differences appear
when Fowler's theory is applied to men, although men tend to
experience a more uneven trajectory of faith development than women.
Quality: Good.   Adds to a growing body of literature on faith
development in later life.

PUBLIC AND PRIVATE BEHAVIORS

Community-Dwelling Elderly

26.   Brennan, C.L. and L.E. Missinne.   1980.   Personal and
       institutionalized religiosity of the elderly. In J.A. Thorson and
       T.C. Cook (eds.), <u>Spiritual Well-Being of the Elderly</u>.
       Springfield, Ill: Charles C. Thomas.
Objective: Examines how older persons in a Midwestern community
view their religious development throughout adulthood, and to
retrospectively assess whether subjects had become more religious
with aging. *Sample & Methods*: 92 persons aged 59 to 93 from three
congregate meal sites and a retirement village completed a
questionnaire about their religious feelings and participation; each
question was asked for the present (currently) and for the past (during
their younger adult years). Subjects were middle-low income and 63%
were women. *Results*: 99% believed in God now and had always
done so; 73% attended church regularly and had always done so; 86%
believed in an afterlife and 84% had always believe this. On the other
hand, 91% considered themselves religious now, although only 72%
had always been so; 83% prayed regularly now, but only 68% had
always done so; and 93% currently felt accepted by other church
members, whereas 83% had always felt so. *Conclusions*: This was
a very religious elderly sample. Although the authors concluded that
religious behavior was relatively stable over the lifespan, there was
evidence that change had indeed occurred - in particular, increasing
subjective religiousness, private prayer, and greater feelings of
acceptance by other members of their church. These are significant
changes in this writer's estimation. *Quality*: Fair.

27.   Ainlay, S.C., and D.R. Smith. 1984.   Aging and religious
       participation. Journal of Gerontology 39:357-363.
Objective: Investigates a multidimensional conception of religious
participation, including organizational and non-organizational activities.
Sample & Methods: 947 persons age 50 or over from five Mennonite
and Brethren in Christ denominations. Respondents categorized into
three age groups: 50-59 (n = 490), 60-69 (n = 261), and 70 or above
(n = 161). Three dimensions of religious participation were examined:
organizational (church attendance, frequency of Sunday school
attendance, attendance at youth or adult meetings, frequency of
serving as Sunday school teacher), attitudes toward organizational
participation (importance of church attendance, interest in attending
Sunday school, interest in serving the home congregation), and non-
organizational activities (private Bible study, private prayer, frequency
of private devotional periods, listening to religious radio programs).
Factor structure of the 11 measures were analyzed and degree to
which the structure varied across the age groups was examined.
Results: Private, non-organizational participation increased while
organizational participation decreased with increasing age.   An
increased homogeneity of religious attitudes and behaviors was found
with increasing age. *Conclusions*: A decline in organizational religious
activity with age is offset by an increase in private religious activities.
Quality: Very good.   One of the first attempts to use structural
equation models to examine the relationship between religious
behaviors and aging.

28.   Young, G., and W. Dowling. 1987.   Dimensions of religiosity in
       old age: Accounting for variation in types of participation.
       Journal of Gerontology 42:376-380.
Objective: Examines the effect of sociodemographic and health factors
on rates of public and private religious activity among older adults.
Sample & Methods: Evaluated 123 elderly West Texans with regard
to social activity, social interaction, health, age, income, religious
conviction, and both public and private religious participation. Multiple
regression analyses tested the hypothesis that religious activity is
compensatory for other deprivations. *Results*: Strength of religious
conviction was the strongest predictor of both public and private
religious behaviors.   Unrelated to private religious activities
(surprisingly) were poor health, low income, functional disability or
living alone. Only strength of the social network predicted higher rates
of private religious activity. *Conclusions*: Elders with well-developed
family and friendship networks are more likely to engage in private
religious activity that may enhance their spiritual well-being. *Quality*:
Good.

29. Payne, B.P. 1988. Religious patterns and participation of older adults: A sociological perspective. Educational Gerontology 14:255-267

Objective: A renowned social gerontologist examines the social profile of religious behaviors in older adults; the effects of aging, period, and cohort effects on socialization to religious practices; and the role that organized religion can play in meeting the needs of older adults. Religious participation is explored using historical and sociological perspectives. *Sample & Methods*: Literature review and discussion. Presents data on church attendance (National Council on Aging 1975) and spiritual commitment (Gallup Polls 1985) for national samples. *Results & Conclusions*: The religiosity of the cohort of elders raised during the first half of the 20th century may be at least partly attributed to their socialization to religion (period effect). Many older adults maintain their religious participation until late life; however, about one-quarter of the elderly disaffiliate or decrease these activities [many may do so because physical disability prevents further active participation]. There are many things that churches can do today to meet the psychosocial needs of their elderly congregants, since churches will be an increasing source of social, physical, and psychological support for older adults in the future. *Quality*: Very Good. It should also be noted that according to yearly Gallup Polls, frequency of church attendance in the United States has changed little since 1935 (hovering around 40% weekly attendance).

30. Chaves, M. 1989. Secularization and religious revival: Evidence from U.S. church attendance rates, 1972-1986. Journal for the Scientific Study of Religion 28 (4):464-477.

Objective: Assesses changes in church attendance over a 15 year period to determine whether Americans are becoming more or less religious over time. *Sample & Methods*: Using data from the National Opinion Research Center, the effects of age, period, and cohort effects on rates of church attendance are examined. The investigator assumed that there were no changes in church attendance after age 70. *Results & Conclusions*: Church attendance remains relatively stable throughout the life course; younger generations are attending church less frequently than are older generations (both Catholics and Protestants); and there appears to have been a revival among Protestants during the early 1980's, with increases in church attendance seen during that period. The coexistence of both secularization and revival is discussed. *Quality*: Good.

31. Payne, B. 1989. Religion and the elderly in today's world. In W.M. Clements (ed), Ministry with the Aging: Designs,

Challenges, Foundations. New York: Haworth Press, pp 153-174.
Objective: The author takes a sociological perspective on religion and the aging process. *Sample & Methods*: Literature review and discussion. *Results & Conclusions*: An examination of the social aspects of religion, patterns of religious participation in later life, and changing demographics of American society has serious implications for churches in this country. *Quality*: Very good.

32. Ainlay, S.C., R. Singleton, and V.L. Swigert. 1992. Aging and religious participation: Reconsidering the effects of health. Journal for the Scientific Study of Religion 31:175-188.

Objective: Examines the relationship between aging and religious involvement, with an emphasis on changes in church attendance, private religious practice, and attitudes toward church involvement. *Sample & Methods*: In 1990, interviews were conducted with a random sample of 229 community-dwelling residents of Worchester, Mass., age 65 or over; 720 residents contacted (32% response rate). Sample consisted of 60% Catholic, 27% Protestant, and 8% Jewish; analysis was limited to Christians (n = 200). Respondents were 98% white and 58% women. *Results*: Age was inversely related to formal religious activities (r = -.22, p < .01), positively related to private religious activities (r = .13), but unrelated to attitudes toward church involvement. Overall physical health condition was inversely related to formal religious participation (r = -.14), but was positively related to private religious activities (r = .16, p < .05). Regression analysis confirmed that functional impairment was inversely related to formal religious activities and church attendance, whereas overall physical condition (number of major health problems, minor complaints, and other health problems) was positively related to private religious activities. *Conclusions*: Health is an important mediating factor in people's late-life religious participation; it explains why many older persons who wish to take part in church life are forced to reduce their participation. The decrease in formal religious involvement is not due to a desire on the part of individuals to "distance" themselves from the church, rather it is declining functional status that prevents such involvement. This finding goes against disengagement theory. *Quality*: Good. Low response rate may affect generalizability.

Community-Dwelling Elderly: Hispanics

33. Delgado, M. 1982. Ethnic and cultural variations in the care of the aged: Hispanic elderly and natural support systems. A

special focus on Puerto Ricans. Journal of Geriatric Psychiatry 15(2):239-251
Objective: Presents an overview of demographic data on Hispanics residing in the United States and examines the key roles of Hispanic elders within human service programs. *Sample & Methods*: No data collected or analyzed. Reviews demographic data presented in New York Times (1979). Discusses four natural support systems including family, folk healers, religion, and merchant and social clubs. Reviews the literature in each of these areas and makes recommendations. *Results & Conclusions*: Hispanic elders perform important natural support functions within the Hispanic community; in particular, they play prominent roles in the religious support system, both as ministers and as members of the congregation. They serve to transmit cultural values (including religion) from one generation to the other. *Quality*: Fair.

34. Guarnaccia, P.J., P. Parra, A. Deschamps, G. Milstein, N. Argiles. 1992. Si dios quiere: Hispanic families' experiences of caring for a seriously mentally ill family member. Culture, Medicine, and Psychiatry 16:187-215.
Objective: Studies Hispanic families' understanding of mental illness, their relationships with mental health professionals, and the burden of caring for seriously mentally ill family members at home. *Sample & Methods*: Based on data collected from Hispanic families in New Jersey. *Results & Conclusions*: Among Hispanics, the family is expected to be the primary caregiver of mentally ill members. The church plays a crucial role in the social support systems of these families; caregivers often receive comfort and solace from beliefs and rituals having to do with religious healing. *Quality*: Good. While not focused primarily on the elderly, the results likely apply equally well to this age group (particularly those with dementia, chronic schizophrenia, etc.).

35. Maldanado, D. 1995. Religion and racial/ethnic minority elderly populations. In M. Kimble, S. McFadden, J. Ellor, & J. Seeber (eds), Aging, Religion, and Spirituality: A Handbook. Minneapolis, MN: Fortress Press
Objective: Examines the role of the church in ethnic minorities, including Hispanic elders. *Sample & Methods*: Unknown. *Results & Conclusions*: The Roman Catholic church among Hispanic elders is the most important social institution in their communities, and their religious faith may be their most significant source of psychological support. *Quality*: Good. One of the few recent pieces that examines the importance of religion in Hispanic elders.

Community-Dwelling Elderly: Blacks

36. Taylor, R.J. 1986. Religious participation among elderly Blacks. Gerontologist 26:630-636.
Objective: Examines religious participation among elderly Blacks. *Sample & Methods*: Nationally representative sample of 581 Blacks age 55 or older surveyed during 1979-1980 (National Survey of Black Americans). Mean age of sample was 67 years; women comprised two-thirds of sample, 39% were married or common law, average family income was $8,000/yr, 10% had some college or a college degree. *Results*: 78% were official members of a church. Five percent attended church every day and an additional 47% attended at least once/week. Female gender and being married were significantly related to church attendance. With regard to subjective religiosity, 59% indicated that they were very religious and another 35% fairly religious; only 1% reported they were not religious at all. *Conclusions*: This research demonstrates that elderly Blacks are frequently church members, have a high rate of church attendance, and often see themselves as very religious. *Quality*: Good. Documents high prevalence of religious activity among elderly Blacks - especially women. See also: Taylor, R.J. 1988. Structural determinants of religious participation among Black Americans. Review of Religious Research 30:114-125.

37. Chatters, L.M., and R.J. Taylor. 1989. Age differences in religious participation among Black adults. Journal of Gerontology 44:S183-S189.
Objective: Examines age differences in private and public religious participation among Black Americans. *Sample & Methods*: Uses data from 2107 participants in the 1979-80 National Survey of Black Americans, a nationally representative cross-sectional sample of adult Blacks (age 18 or older) in the United States. Regression models were constructed for men and women separately, controlling for marital status, income, education, urbanicity, region, and health disability. *Results*: In both men and women, there is a near linear increase in private (prayer, reading religious materials), church-related activities, and subjective religiosity from young adulthood to age 74; there is a slight dropoff in church attendance and reading religious materials after age 75, although frequency of prayer and subjective religiosity continue to increase. There is a slightly stronger relationship between age and reading religious materials in women than in men, and a slightly stronger correlation between age and frequency of prayer in men than in women. *Conclusions*: This research demonstrates the rather marked difference in frequency of religious behaviors and attitudes among older

compared with younger Black Americans. Whether this is a cohort or an aging effect, is unknown. *Quality*: Very Good.

38. Taylor, R.J., and L.M. Chatters. 1991. Nonorganizational religious participation among elderly Black adults. Journal of Gerontology 46:S103-S111.

Objective: Investigates prevalence of nonorganizational religious activities (reading religious literature, watching or listening to religious programs, prayer or requests for prayer) among elderly Blacks. *Sample & Methods*: Representative cross-sectional survey of 581 Black adults age 55 or over in the continental U.S. (National Survey of Black Americans) conducted by the Institute of Social Research at University of Michigan; sample characteristics were 63% women, 39% married/common law, $5,000/yr income (median), and 8 years education (median). *Results*: 44% of respondents read religious books and materials nearly every day and an additional 24% read them at least weekly; 34% listen to or watch religious programs nearly every day and an additional 50% listen to them at least weekly; 94% pray nearly every day; 18% ask others to pray for them nearly every day and another 24% ask others at least weekly to pray for them. Gender (women) was the strongest predictor of participation in nonreligious activities. Age was the second strongest predictor of frequency of prayer, with older Blacks praying more than younger Blacks. Educational level (lower) predicted frequency of listening to or watching religious programs. Health disability was associated with frequency of watching or listening to religious programs, with the latter activity presumably compensating for an inability to participate in formal religious activities. *Conclusions*: The prevalence of private religious activities among older Blacks (especially women) is very high. These findings have implications for social and health care professionals who work with older Black Americans, and suggest the need to include non-organizational activities in any conceptualization of religiosity in older Blacks. *Quality*: Very Good. A remarkable report - almost half of the entire sample reading religious books and materials every day.

39. Chatters, L.M., J.S. Levin, and R.J. Taylor. 1992. Antecedents and dimensions of religious involvement among older Black adults. Journal of Gerontology 47:S269-S278.

Objective: A psychometric paper which proposes and tests a measurement model of religiosity in elderly Blacks. *Sample and Methods*: Uses data from a sample of 581 Black Americans age 55 or over (National Survey of Black Americans, 1979-80). LISREL VI was used to examine the "fit" of a model that incorporated three dimensions of religiosity: organizational, nonorganizational, and subjective religiosity. *Results*: The proposed model provided a good fit to the data. While there were few differences among older adults in relation to organizational and non-organizational religiosity, background factors such as age (older), gender (female), region (southern), family income (low), and education (low) all predicted greater subjective religiosity. *Conclusions*: A measurement model for conceptualizing and studying religiosity in older Blacks was confirmed. Sociodemographic factors were differentially related to the three religious constructs comprising the model. *Quality*: Very high. Confirms statistically what conventional wisdom would dictate.

40. Levin, J.S., and R.J. Taylor. 1993. Gender and age differences in religiosity among Black Americans. Gerontologist 33(1):16-23.
Objective: Examines differences in religiosity among elderly Blacks based on age and gender. *Sample & Methods*: Over a dozen religious variables were examined in this nationally representative sample of 2,107 Black Americans (National Study of Black Americans). *Results*: Women far exceeded men in levels of religiosity at all ages, even after accounting for variables such as education, marital and employment status, region of the country, urbanicity, and health satisfaction. *Conclusions*: Once again, elderly Black women are the most religious element in our society. *Quality*: Very Good.

41. Levin, J.S., R.J. Taylor, and L.M. Chatters. 1994. Race and gender differences in religiosity among older adults: Findings from four national surveys. Journal of Gerontology 49:S137- S145.
Objective: Examines racial and gender differences in religiosity among older adults. *Sample & Methods*: Data from four national surveys (Quality of American Life survey, Myth and Reality of Aging survey, Americans' Changing Lives survey, and General Social Survey [1987]) were used. Measures of organizational, non-organizational, and subjective religiosity were present in the four surveys. *Results & Conclusions*: Significant racial and gender differences were found in all four surveys, despite controlling for age, education, marital status, income, region, urbanicity, and subjective health. Women and Blacks consistently showed higher religiosity than men or Whites. *Quality*: Excellent. Reflects what Gallup Polls have been showing for the general population.

Clinical Populations

42. Adams, R.G., and J.L. Brittain. 1987. Journal of Religion and
     Aging 3 (3-4):35-48.
Objective: Examines how functional impairment affects church
attendance among the rural elderly. Sample & Methods: 412 adults
age 60 or over comprised the sample for this study. Five dimensions
of functional impairment were examined: physical health, mental
health, SES, ability to perform ADLs, and social resources (Duke OARS
methodology). Results & Conclusions: It is important to examine
measures of functional impairment, in addition to age, when assessing
changes in church participation across the life cycle. Recommendations are made to help facilitate the participation of older adults in the
religious community. Quality: Good.

See also:

8. Koenig et al. 1988. Journal of the American Geriatrics Society
   36:362-374.
9. Bearon & Koenig. 1990. The Gerontologist 30:249-253.

SUBJECTIVE RELIGIOUS EXPERIENCE

Community-Dwelling Elderly

43. Johnson, D., S. Williams, and D. Bromley. 1986. Religion, health,
     and healing: Findings from a Southern city. Sociological
     Analysis 47(1):66-73.
Objective: Investigates the prevalence of faith healing - healing that
could be attributed to prayer or regarded as a divine healing. Sample
& Methods: Random digit dialing was used to contact 586 adult
residents of Richmond, Virginia in 1984. Included in the study was the
following question: "Have you ever experienced a healing of a serious
disease or physical condition that you believed resulted from prayer or
considered to be a divine healing?". Results: 14% of the total sample
responded in the affirmative (11% of those under age 30, 12% ages
30-49, 21% ages 50-64, and 16% of those over age 65). The most
common category of healing was a cold/flu (12%); 7% (n = 12)
reported healings of tumors or cancers. Conclusions: Prevalence of
faith healings increased with age, such that 19.5% of persons age 50
or over reported such healings. Quality: Fair to Good. Interesting
finding that one out of five older adults have had these experiences.

44. Levin, J.S. 1993. Age differences in mystical experience. The Gerontologist 33:507-513.

Objective: Examines age differences in reports of deja vu, ESP, clairvoyance, spiritualism, and other numinous experiences. *Sample & Methods*: Data from 1481 participants of the 1988 General Social Survey (GSS, a representative national survey) were examined for reports of mystical experiences. *Results*: Compared to data gathered in 1973, mystical experiences were more common in the 1988 survey. A composite mysticism score, generated from several questions on the GSS, was found to increase with successively younger age cohorts (e.g., mystical experiences were less commonly reported by older adults). Levin also found that while personal or subjective religiosity was positively related to mystical experiences, organizational religiosity (e.g., church attendance) was *inversely* related. *Conclusions*: Mystical experiences (non-traditional) are more common among younger age cohorts, and are inversely related to socially-oriented religious participation. *Quality*: Good.

Clinical Populations

45. Koenig, H.G. 1994. Religious conversion (Ch 19). In H.G. Koenig, Aging and God. NY: Haworth Press, pp 419-438.

Objective: Examines the prevalence of life-changing religious experiences among elderly men hospitalized with medical illnesses. *Sample & Methods*: 1010 consecutive patients under age 40 and over age 65 years admitted to the medical or neurological services of the Durham (North Carolina) VA hospital were asked if they had ever experienced a distinct change in their feelings about religion. *Results*: Over one-half of younger men (54%) and one-third of elderly men (33%) reported such experiences, over 85% of which were positive, life-changing, and faith strengthening. When asked at what age they had the experience, 42% of men age 65 or over indicated that they had it after they turned 50 years old. The oldest age when such an experience was reported was 82, and that patient had it during the study period while he was in ICU. *Conclusions*: Many younger and older adults have had life-changing religious experiences, most of which are positive and life-enhancing. For older men, almost half of these experiences were reported to occur after the age of 50 - often occur during stressful life periods (while coming off of an alcohol addiction, during wartime, or other difficult situation); health problems were the precipitating event in about 15% of cases. One of the few studies that has employed a random, systematically selected sample of elderly patients to study this phenomenon; note, however, that all patients were middle or lower class men living in the Southeastern United States.

USE OF RELIGION TO COPE

Community-Dwelling Elderly

46. Rosen, C.E. 1982. Ethnic differences among impoverished rural elderly in use of religion as a coping mechanism. Journal of Rural Community Psychology 3(2):27-34.
Objective: Examines use of religion as a coping behavior among a group of impoverished elderly at high risk for emotional disorder. *Sample & Methods*: Standardized clinical interviews were conducted by mental health professionals with 148 subjects age 65 years or over who attended senior centers in small communities surrounding Athens, Georgia. *Results*: 40% of respondents indicated that they used religion to cope with stress; 26% indicated that they used it to reduce feelings of depression.   Blacks used religion much more often than did impoverished Whites. The authors suggest that this might explain why Blacks, despite their unfavorable circumstances, evaluated their past life and their future more positively than did Whites. *Conclusion*: The high prevalence of religious coping among Blacks have implications for intervention programs for the elderly in rural areas (i.e., role of the church). *Quality*: Good.

47. Manfredi, C., and M. Pickett. 1987. Perceived stressful situations and coping strategies utilized by the elderly.   Journal of Community Health Nursing 4(2):99-110.
Objective: Examines the types of stressful situations experienced by the elderly and the coping strategies they implement to deal with that stress.   *Sample & Methods*: Data was gather from a convenience sample of 51 adults age 60 or over; subjects resided in senior center housing complexes in southern Rhode Island (82% female, 60% spouse deceased, 71% completed high school, race unknown). Subjects were asked to describe a stressful event they had experienced within the past month, and how they had coped with that stress. *Results & Conclusions*: Loss and conflict were the two major types of stress experienced; prayer was the most frequently used coping strategy. *Quality*: Fair.

48. Koenig, H.G., L.K. George, and I.C. Siegler. 1988. The use of religion and other emotion-regulating coping strategies among

older adults. <u>The Gerontologist</u> 28:303-310.
Objective: Explores how older adults (all White, middle-upper socioeconomic class) coped with (1) the most stressful event in their life, (2) the most stressful event in the past 10 years, and (3) the most stressful experience in the present. *Sample & Methods*: Stratified random sample of 100 older participants in the Duke Longitudinal Study of Aging (II); subjects originally chosen from the membership roster of the Blue Cross-Blue Shield Insurance program in central North Carolina. Subjects were 50% men and 50% women; mean age was 67 years; average educational level was at least some college; 73% were married and 90% were from a Protestant background. Open ended questions were asked about how participants coped with the three event-periods noted above; responses were tape-recorded and categorized. *Results*: A total of 556 coping strategies were spontaneously offered by the 100 participants; the most common coping behavior was religious in nature (17%). Religious responses were mentioned 45% of the time for at least one of the three stressful periods inquired about; they were more commonly offered by women than men (58% vs 32%). Three-quarters (74%) of religious responses had to do with placing trust or faith in God, praying, or obtaining help and strength from God (cognitive responses). *Conclusions*: Religious coping was the most commonly used strategy for dealing with stress in this sample of well-educated and financially secure older adults; religious cognitions (trust, faith, prayer) - rather than the social aspects of religion - were most frequently mentioned.

49.   Pargament, K.I., J. Kennell, W. Hathaway, N. Grevengoed, J. Newman, and W. Jones. 1988. Religion and the problem-solving process: Three styles of coping. <u>Journal for the Scientific Study of Religion</u> 27:90-104.
Objective: Three styles of religious coping were proposed based on the person's relationship with and perception of God. These were then related to personal competence. *Sample & Methods*: 197 persons drawn from a Presbyterian and a Missouri-Lutheran church in the midwest (average age 46, 57% women, 100% white). The three religious coping styles were self-directing, deferring, and collaborative. Personal competence was measured in terms of three dimensions: self attitude, world-attitude, and active problem solving. *Results & Conclusions*: The self-directing approach may be most useful for people dealing with situations that are under their control; in situations which cannot be altered by personal action (like chronic medical illness), a deferring approach may be more helpful. *Quality*: Very good. While this study was conducted in a relatively young sample, its results are relevant to older adults. Physical disability may cause some older

adults to abandon a self-directing coping style (based on God's allowance of individuals to solve their own problems) to prefer a more deferring style where the person is more dependent on God's grace.

50. Jackson, J.S., T.C. Antonucci, and R.C. Gibson. 1990. Cultural, racial, and ethnic minority influences on aging. In J.E. Birren, K.W. Schaie (eds.), Handbook of the Psychology of Aging (3rd ed), pp 103-123. San Diego: Academic Press

Objective: Reviews the literature, including the influences of religion on aging among minority elders. *Sample & Methods*: Literature review. *Results & Conclusions*: Religion is particularly important in the lives of Blacks and other minority elders. Quality: Good.

See also:

77. Koenig et al. (1989). Journal of Religion and Aging 5(4):73.
80. Koenig et al. (1990). International Journal of Geriatric Psychiatry 5:123.

Clinical Populations

51. Conway, K. 1985-86. Coping with the stress of medical problems among Black and White elderly. International Journal of Aging and Human Development 21(1):39-48.

Objective: Explores the coping responses of urban elderly women to the stressful event of a medical problem. *Sample & Methods*: 200 women aged 65 years or older were randomly selected from a pool of 650 women living in low-income elderly housing projects in Kansas City, Kansas; 93 of subjects consented; 65 completed inperson interviews lasting 1-4 hrs. Sample composed of 58% Blacks, 42% White, mean age 78 yrs, 82% widowed. A list of action-oriented and cognitive-oriented coping responses [to medical problems] was provided to respondents who noted yes or no. *Results*: The five most common action-oriented behaviors were pray (91%), see doctor (89%), use medications (75%), seek information (72%), rest (71%), or stay at home (71%); most common cognitive-oriented coping behaviors were think of religion (86%), compare to others worse off (86%), positive attitude (will manage 72% or have to get through 60%), and problem solving (52%). When asked who assisted them when facing a stressful medical problem, 85% responded "God" (compared with 78% responding "Professional"). Religious coping was more common in Blacks than Whites (pray 97% vs 81%; think of religion 95% vs 74%). *Conclusions*: Religious forms of coping are common in this population, especially in elderly Blacks. *Quality*: Fair.

52. Koenig, H.G. 1988. Case studies (Ch 9). In H.G. Koenig, M.
    Smiley, and J.P. Gonzales (eds.), Religion, Health, and Aging.
    Westport, CT: Greenwood Press, pp 103-118.
Objective: Examines cases of older persons using religion as a coping
resource. *Sample & Methods*: Thirteen cases are presented and
discussed. Most cases involve physically ill older persons. *Results &
Conclusions*: Some older persons almost exclusively use religion to deal
and cope with stressful life changes, particularly those brought on by
physical illness. Illustrates in a qualitative manner what quantitative
studies are showing. Also see reference 55.

53. Weinrich, S., S.B. Hardin, M. Johnson. 1990. Nurses respond
    to Hurricane Hugo victims' disaster stress. Archives of
    Psychiatric Nursing 4:1955-205.
Objective: Examines student nurses' reports of how victims of
Hurricane Hugo coped with this natural disaster. *Sample & Methods*:
38 of 61 student nurses from the University of South Carolina
completed a Disaster Stress Questionnaire that assessed, along with
other things, the victims' coping skills. *Results*: The most frequently
reported coping strategy identified by nurses was "talking about Hugo"
(95% of nurses reported this); the second most common coping
strategy was "humor" (82%); and the third most commmon coping
behavior was religion (74%). *Conclusions*: For our purposes, the most
relevant conclusion was that 74% of nurses reported that victims used
religion as a primary coping strategy. *Quality*: Fair. Of interest, since
few objective studies have examined coping responses to natural
disasters.

54. Koenig, H.G., H.J. Cohen, D.G. Blazer, C. Pieper, K.G. Meador,
    F. Shelp, V. Goli, and R. DiPasquale. 1992. Religious coping
    and depression among elderly, hospitalized medically ill men.
    American Journal of Psychiatry 149:1693-1700.
Objective: Examines the prevalence and correlates of religious coping
in hospitalized elderly male veterans [depression relationship reviewed
in Section II]. *Sample & Methods*: 850 consecutively admitted men
age 65 or over to the medical and neurological services (77% response
rate); mean age 70 years, 28% Black, mean education 9 yrs, 68%
married. Religious Coping Index administered to all patients. *Results*:
20% (24% of those age 70 years or over) spontaneously gave a
religious response to an open-ended coping question, indicating that
religion was the most important factor that kept them going; 56%
rated themselves at 7.5 or higher (large extent or more) on a 0 to 10

visual analogue scale indicating how much religion was used to help them to cope. A regression model revealed that the strongest correlates of religious coping were Black race, high social support, a family history of psychiatric problems, abstinence from alcohol, and Black Protestant or fundamentalist religious denomination. *Conclusions*: Religious coping is common among older men when faced with serious, life-threatening medical problems. [See Part II for review of this articles findings with regard to the relationship with depression.]

55. Koenig, H.G. 1994. Using religion to cope (Ch 9). In H.G. Koenig, Aging and God. New York: Haworth Press, pp 161-187.

Objective: One of the aims was to assess changes in religiosity with age. *Sample & Methods*: Approximately 450 consecutive patients under age 40 and over age 70 years (68%) admitted to the medical or neurological services of the Durham (North Carolina) VA hospital. Each patients was asked if his religious faith had increased, decreased, or stayed the same as they had grown older. *Results*: The majority (60%) reported that religion had become more important as they had grown older, 35% indicated it had remained the same, and 5% said it had decreased. Age had little effect on the distribution of responses; for men under age 40, 54% indicated it had increased in importance, 40% remained the same, and 6% decreased. *Conclusions*: The majority of men with health problem severe enough to require hospitalization, report that the importance of religion has increased for them as they've grown older. See Glamser 1987 above (ref 1) for information on community sample.

56. Koenig, H.G. 1994. Cases of religious coping in action (Ch 10). In H.G. Koenig, Aging and God. New York: Haworth Press, pp 189-217.

Objective: Explores the religious coping responses of younger and older patients hospitalized with medical illness. *Sample & Methods*: Consecutively admitted patients to a VA medical center were asked to explain what factors enabled them to cope with the stresses in their lives (including physical illness). Of 1011 men admitted and questioned, 97 met the criteria specified for "strong religious copers" (8% of those under age 40 and 10% of those over age 65). Religious responses (both spontaneous and elicited) are given verbatim for each of the 97 cases. *Results & Conclusions*: Presents nearly 100 systematically collected verbatim reports of how young and older men use religion as a coping resource. There are numerous similarities and differences in the way younger and older persons use religion to cope when hospitalized with life-threatening physical illness.

See also:

113. O'Brien, M.E. 1982. J Religion and Health 21:68.
115. Spiegel, D., J.R. Bloom, and E. Gottheil. 1983. Psychosocial
       Oncology 1(1):33.
119. Idler, E.L. 1987. Social Forces 66:226.
124. Pressman, P., J.S. Lyons, D.B. Larson, and J.J. Strain. 1990. Am
       J Psychiatry 147:758.
129. Koenig, H.G., H.J. Cohen, D.G. Blazer, and K.R.R. Krishnan.
       1995. Psychosomatics, in press.
148. Hall, G.R., and B.L. Grandquist. 1989. Iowa Task Force Report,
       p 115.
149. Rabins, P.V., M.D. Fitting, J. Esatham, and J. Zabora. 1990. Age
       and Aging 19:185.
150. Wood, J.B., and, I.A. Parham. 1990. J Applied Gerontology
       9:325-329.
151. Whitlatch, A.M., D.I. Meddaugh, and K.J. Langhout. 1992. Am
       J of ADRD and Research, Nov-Dec:11.
175. Yates, J., B. Chalmer, P. St. James, M. Follansbee, and F.
       McKegnery. 1981. Medical and Pediatric Oncology 9:121.

Part II

Relationships Between Religion and Health

RELIGION AND MENTAL HEALTH

Life Satisfaction (community studies)

57.   Toseland, R., and J. Rasch. 1979-80. Correlates of life satisfaction: An AID analysis. <u>International Journal of Aging and Human Development</u> 10:203-211.

Objective: The Automatic Interaction Detector (AID3) was used to develop a model of factors predicting life satisfaction in a sample of older adults; focus is not on religion per se, but includes a religious predictor in the analysis. *Sample & Methods*: Data come from a subset of a random national sample of teenagers and adults living in 28 communities across the United States; 871 persons were age 55 or older, and they comprise the sample for this report. A 90 minute interview was conducted with each respondent in Spring 1973. Sample characteristics were 51% ages 55 to 65, 56% female, 72% married, and median income $10,000-$14,999/yr. Thirty-one demographic, community, and social-psychological variables were included in this analysis. Religious participation was one of those variables, although there was no indication of how it was measured. *Results*: The strongest predictors of life satisfaction were family life satisfaction and personal health satisfaction; religious participation was unrelated to overall life satisfaction. *Conclusions*: Family and personal health satisfaction are the primary predictors of overall predictors of life satisfaction. *Quality*: Fair. One of the few "no association" studies in the literature. It is not surprising that satisfaction with family and health are strongly related to overall life satisfaction; indeed, conventional wisdom would suggest that life satisfaction would be largely based on these other satisfactions. What is not clear, however, is the role that religious participation may have played in causing satisfaction with family and health.

58. Shaver, P., M. Lenauer, and S. Sadd. 1980. Religiousness, conversion, and subjective well-being: The "healthy-minded" religion of modern American women. American Journal of Psychiatry 137:1563-1568.

Objective: Examined how religiousness was related to self-reported mental and physical well-being, and to what extent religiousness had changed over the past 5 years. *Sample & Methods*: Random sample of 2,500 responses taken from 65,000 self-selected replies by women to a 97-item questionnaire published in Redbook in 1976. Ages ranged from 15 to 91 (mean 35); 23% were Catholic and 70% Protestant. Compared to American women in general, sample was better educated (60% had more than a high school education) and were more likely to be White (96%). The questionnaire assessed religious beliefs and experiences; respondents were also asked if they had become more or less religious over the past 5 years. Mental health was measured by the question: "In general, how happy or unhappy have you been in the last six months?" (7 response options). *Results*: Women who were either very religious or antireligious scored lowest on the unhappiness scale; those who were only slightly religious reported the most unhappiness. This curvilinear response was also true for headaches, loss of sexual interest, feelings of loneliness, stomach upset, crying easily, worry or anxiety, irrational fears, restless sleep, feelings of worthlessness, guilt, and tenseness. *Conclusions*: Slightly religious respondents (ambivalent?) were less happy and more depressed than either the very religious or the anti-religious. 58% indicated that they had become more religious in the past 5 years, whereas 28% had stayed about the same, and 9% became less religious. *Quality*: Fair. Highly select sample (readers of Redbook magazine); analyses were not controlled for relevant confounders.

59. Steinitz, L.Y. 1980. Religiosity, well-being, and Weltanschauung among the elderly. Journal for the Scientific Study of Religion 19:60-67.

Objective: Examines how well religion predicts personal well-being, life satisfaction, and world view in the elderly. *Sample & Methods*: Data drawn from responses of community-dwelling persons age 65 or over surveyed by the National Opinion Research Center (NORC) between 1972-1977. Four religious variables were correlated with thirteen self-report items on well-being, life satisfaction, and world view. *Results & Conclusions*: Only one of four religious variables (belief in life after death) was significantly correlated with well-being. *Quality*: Good. One of the few "no [or minimal] association" studies in the literature.

60. Costa, P.T., R.R. McCrae, and A.H. Norris. 1981. Personal adjustment to aging: Longitudinal prediction from neuroticism and extraversion. Journal of Gerontology 36:78-85.

Objective: Examines temperament factors (neuroticism, extraversion, and thinking introversion) as predictors of well-being and adjustment to aging. *Sample & Methods*: This was a 17 year longitudinal study of 557 men aged 17-97 years sponsored by the National Institute on Aging. *Results*: Well-being and adjustment was inversely related to neuroticism and positively related to extraversion in both younger and older persons. Positive attitudes toward religion was related to "thinking introversion." *Conclusions*: Enduring temperamental traits (like extraversion) predict personal adjustment and well-being in later life. *Quality*: Good (methodology very good). Refer to article for discussion about religion-thinking introversion relationship.

61. Beckman, L.J., and B.B. Houser. 1982. The consequences of childlessness on the social-psychological well-being of older women. Journal of Gerontology 37:243-250.

Objective: Examines the effects of childlessness on the well-being of older women, including a number of religious variables as covariables. *Sample & Methods*: A complex 2-stage random sampling method was used to identify potential subjects. Interviews were conducted with 719 white Los Angeles County women between ages 60 and 75 (mean 69); half were married and living with spouse; half of the sample were currently childless and half had living children. Four groups resulted: married childless, widowed childless, married parent, widowed parent. Philadelphia Geriatric Center Morale Scale was used to assess well-being, the outcome variable. Hierarchical regression models were used in the analysis. *Results*: Among "childless married," being unemployed, physically ill, or being Jewish was related to lower levels of well-being. Among "childless widowed," having a low physical capacity was related to lower well-being, whereas quality of social interaction and self-rated religiosity were related to higher well-being. Among "parent married," being Protestant, having a high level of education, and quality of social interaction were all related to higher well-being. Among "parent widowed," being Protestant, having a large number of sisters, and having high subjective religiosity were related to higher well-being, whereas being physically ill and having more social contacts were related to low well-being. *Conclusions*: After other variables were controlled, both religious background and subjective religiosity were important variables related to well-being in these older women.

Quality: Very Good; one of the few studies from the West coast.

62. Singh, B.K., and J.S. Williams. 1982. Satisfaction with health and physical condition among the elderly. Journal of Psychiatric Treatment and Evaluation 4:403-408.

Objective: Examines satisfaction with health and physical conditions among community-dwelling elderly. *Sample & Methods*: Data for study came from six national surveys conducted by the Nation Opinion Research Center (NORC) between 1973 and 1978. This nationally representative sample consisted of 1,459 persons age 65 or over. *Results*: Regardless of which data set was used to assess the relationship, religious attendance was significantly related to satisfaction with health (p<.001), a relationship which persisted in significance after controlling for other factors. In fact, attendance at religious services was the strongest predictor of satisfaction, followed by education, working status, and race. *Conclusion*: Authors note that more frequent church attendance might create a greater sense of well being, and thus greater satisfaction with health and life in general. Direction of causation, of course, cannot be proven from these data. *Quality*: Good.

63. Tellis-Nayak, V. 1982. The transcendent standard: The religious ethos of the rural elderly. The Gerontologist 22:359-363.

Objective: Explores the relationship between religiosity and feelings of loneliness, anxiety about death, meaning in life, and general psychic well-being. *Sample & Methods*: Random sample of 259 persons age 60 or older from a small town in rural upstate New York; characteristics of the sample include white (96%), female (64%), registered voters (84%), relatively well-educated, and a median yearly income of $6,300. Predominant religious affiliations were Catholic (26%), Methodist (26%), Baptists (17%), and Presbyterians (12%). Religiosity was measured by combining scores on single items measuring the four dimensions of ideology, ritual, experience, and consequence. *Results*: While religiosity was only weakly related to loneliness, psychic well-being, and death anxiety, it was strongly related to "meaning in life," accounting for 24% of the variance and 90% of the explained variance for that construct. *Conclusion*: The author concludes that religion provides the older person with a "guiding and comprehensive view" of life which transforms everyday reality, infusing it with meaning and motivation. *Quality*: Good.

64. Markides, K.S. 1983. Aging, religiosity, and adjustment: A longitudinal analysis. Journal of Gerontology 38:621-625.

Objective: Assesses relations between church attendance, prayer, and self-rated religiosity, life-satisfaction, and aging over a 4 year period in person age 60 or over. *Sample & Methods*: 551 Mexican-Americans (mean age 70 years) from San Antonio, Texas, were surveyed in 1976 and 336 of these (66%) were surveyed again in 1980; 70% were Mexican-Americans and 60% were women. Life satisfaction was measured by Neugarten's Life Satisfaction Index. Analyses were controlled for education, health, marital status, and age, using regression models. *Results*: Church attendance and private prayer remained relatively stable over the 4 years of the study, while self-rated religiosity increased. Only church attendance was significantly related to life-satisfaction for both Mexican-Americans and Anglos. Among Anglos, this relationship increased significantly from 1976 to 1980. *Conclusions*: The findings provide partial support for the notion that religiosity is a significant independent predictor of life-satisfaction, and that this relationship increases with age. *Quality*: Very good. See later followup study Markides et al. 1988 reference below (ref #71).

65.   West, G.E., and R.L. Simons.   1983. Sex differences in stress, coping resources, and illness among the elderly. Research on Aging 5:235-268.

Objective: Same study as Simons & West 1984-85, except that they divide sample by sex and examine gender differences in the relationships. *Sample & Methods*: Described previously. *Results & Conclusions*: Religiosity was unrelated to number of physical illnesses, and did not buffer the effects of stressful life events on inducing physical illness. Again, this study did not measure or address the question of whether religion helped older persons psychologically cope with or adjust better to physical illness or stressful life events. *Quality*: Fair. See comments in Simons & West 1984-85 reference below (ref 66).

66.   Simons, R.L., and G.E. West. 1984-1985. Life changes, coping resources, and health among the elderly. International Journal of Aging and Human Development 20:173-189.

Objective: Examines the extent to which social network involvement, marital status, occupational status, income, and religion buffer the effect of stressful life events on the number of physical illnesses experienced by older persons within the past year. *Sample & Methods*: A population of 7,000 elderly persons was identified in Ames, Iowa; 325 men and 300 women were randomly sampled from this population. A questionnaire was mailed out and followed up by a letter. Fifty-one percent of potential subjects responded, yielding a sample of 308 persons; usable data for this analysis was available on 299 respondents, 132 men and 167 women. Median income was

$10,200/yr, and 23% of the sample was working full or part-time; 96% of respondents were city-dwellers. Included in the questionnaire were the Geriatric Schedule of Recent Experience, Seriousness of Illness Rating Scale, a 5-item self-efficacy scale, a social resources scale, and a 4-item religiosity scale (religious commitment, prayer, reading religious materials, and experience of God's presence). *Results*: Number of physical illnesses was positively correlated with number of life events, but not with any other variables (including religiosity). When interactions between coping resources and number of life events were examined (to assess their buffering capacity), only occupational status and income buffered between number of life events and number of physical illnesses. Conclusions: Neither religiosity or other social resources buffer the effects of life change on physical illness. *Quality*: Fair. Excessively vague use of the term "coping resource". Assumes that coping outcome can be measured in terms of numbers of physical illnesses experienced in past year. Does not examine whether coping resources actually helped elders to adjust better psychologically to their physical conditions.

67. Cole, T.R. 1984. Aging, meaning and well-being: Musings of a cultural historian. International Journal of Aging and Human Development 19:329-336.
Objective: Author reflects on social integration and well-being of the elderly. *Sample & Methods*: Discussion based on the author's review of 1,000 Protestants sermons delivered between 1800 and 1900. *Results & Conclusions*: Two models of growing old were set up as ideals in the 19th Century, the Calvinistic and civilized models, which depict aging as a spiritual journey. With the growth of science and technology and emphasis on productivity, these ideals have become influential, with a more negative view of aging taking their place. *Quality*: Good.

68. Hall, C.M. 1985. Religion and aging. Journal of Religion and Health 24(1):70-78.
Objective: Examines the role that religion has in the lives of older adults and their families. *Sample & Methods*: Qualitative life-history data are gathered from 500 families to examine religious beliefs that can lead to greater meaning and quality of life for older persons. *Results & Conclusions*: Religion can be used to address concerns that persons have in later life, and thus lead to greater life satisfaction and purpose. *Quality*: Fair.

69. Hunsberger, B. 1985. Religion, age, life satisfaction, and perceived sources of religiousness: A study of older persons.

Journal of Gerontology 40:615-620.
Objective: Examines whether religiosity increases with age and whether
it is related to health and/or life satisfaction; also assesses self-
perceived sources of religiousness during childhood from primary family
members or other sources. *Sample & Methods*: 85 patients aged 65
to 88 living around Ontario, Canada, were recruited and paid to
participate in the study; sample was composed of 61% women and
39% men. The data were retrospective self-reports of perceived
religiousness and changes over time. Christian orthodoxy (using
Christian Orthodoxy Scale), religious socialization, and attitudes on
religious issues were assessed. Religiousness was plotted for each 10-
year interval of subjects' lives. *Results*: Trend analysis demonstrated
a significant linear trend (p < .01) towards increasing religiousness with
age; when stratified by Christian orthodoxy, those who were highly
orthodox reported that their religiousness had increased with time,
whereas those who scored low on orthodoxy demonstrated an opposite
trend toward decreasing religiousness over time. Christian orthodoxy,
background religious emphasis, importance of beliefs, and church
attendance were all significantly associated with happiness and
adjustment. Sources of religiousness included (in order of most
importance) mother, church, father, reading, habit, and personal
experience. *Conclusions*: There is a general tendency towards
increased religiosity with aging, particularly among the highly religious,
which appears to be associated with both life satisfaction and
subjective health. *Quality*: Good.

70.   Usui, W.M., T.J. Keil, and K.R. Durig. 1985. Socioeconomic
      comparisons and life satisfaction of elderly adults. Journal of
      Gerontology 40:110-114.
Objective: Tested the hypothesis that overall satisfaction with life is
strongly influenced by one's financial situation compared with that of
significant others. *Sample & Methods*: 704 adults age 60 or over
randomly sampled from Jefferson County, Kentucky, in 1980. Life
satisfaction measured with Neurgarten Index. *Results*: Life
satisfaction was greatest among respondents who perceived
themselves to be better financially off than the relative to whom they
felt the closest. Church attendance was among the six top predictors
of life satisfaction, after income and other variables were accounted
for. *Conclusions*: No mention of the church attendance - life
satisfaction relationship was mentioned, given that this was not the
focus of the report. *Quality*: Good.

71. Markides, K.S., J.S. Levin, and L.A. Ray. 1987. Religion, aging,
    and life satisfaction: An eight-year, three-wave longitudinal

study. The Gerontologist 27:660-665.

Objective: Takes another look at the relations between religiosity (church attendance, prayer, self-rated religiosity), life satisfaction, and aging, this time including data from wave III (1984) of the longitudinal study noted above. *Sample*: Subjects included in the analysis were 230 of the original 510 subjects (45%) who were surveyed at all three time points (1976, 1980, 1984). Patients who dropped out (55% of the sample) were more likely to be physically ill, and more likely to attend church less because of their health problems. *Results & Conclusions*: This time, little evidence was found to support the notion that older people turn increasingly to religion as they age, decline in health, and face death; nor did they confirm their earlier finding that religiosity increasingly predicted life satisfaction with age. When all respondents (including dropouts) were included in the analyses, however, church attendance was a significant predictor of life-satisfaction; when dropouts were excluded, it lost its significance. *Quality*: Very good, with qualifications. This study demonstrates the impact that dropouts can have on analyses in multi-wave studies; note that only 45% of the original subjects completed all three phases of the study. Those who dropped out were more likely to have progressive physical illness - precisely that group in which private prayer and personal indicators of religiosity might become increasingly important and relevant for maintaining life-satisfaction. Thus, excluding this important group of respondents could mask the association between increasing age, religiosity, and life satisfaction.

72.   Cox, H. and A. Hammonds. 1988. Religiosity, aging, and life satisfaction. Journal of Religion and Aging 5(1/2):1-21.

Objective: Reviews research examining changes with aging in church attendance, belief in God, and belief in an afterlife, and assesses the relationship between religiosity and life satisfaction. *Sample & Methods*: Literature review and discussion. *Results*: Church attendance is low between ages 18-24, remains stable between ages 25 and 54, rises after 54 until age 80 and then drops slightly (due to health). The older one is, the more likely the person is to believe in God and in life after death. All studies looking ar religiosity and life satisfaction have found that church attendance and life satisfaction are correlated. The positive functions of the church in the lives of older adults are discussed and linked with theory. *Conclusions*: Both the social and personal/private aspects of religion play a greater role among older than younger adults. Church attendance, in particular, is linked with greater life satisfaction and personal adjustment in late life. *Quality*: Good. Provides summary tables that demonstrate trends with age and denominational affiliation.

73. Koenig, H.G., J.N. Kvale, and C. Ferrel. 1988. Religion and well-being in later life. The Gerontologist 28:18-28.

Objective: Examines the relationship between well-being and three religious measures (organizational religious activity, private religious activity, and intrinsic religiosity), while controlling for health, social support, and economic status. *Sample & Methods*: A purposive sample of 836 community-dwelling older adults (mean age 73.4 years) completed a the short-version of the Springfield Religiosity Schedule and the Philadelphia Geriatric Center Morale Scale. Subjects were recruited from senior centers in Illinois, Missouri, and Iowa, from church-goers, geriatric medicine clinic participants, and retired nuns in Springfield, Illinois. *Results*: There was a moderate to strong positive relationship between public, private, and intrinsic religious involvement, and well-being in this sample. Religious behaviors and attitudes were particularly strong correlates of morale for women and those 75 years or over. For participants age 75 or older, only self-rated health accounted for more of the explained variance in well-being than did religious variables. *Conclusions*: Religious activities and attitudes appear to influence the complex interaction of health and sociodemographic factors on morale and well-being in later life.

74. Levin, J.S., and K.S. Markides. 1988. Religious attendance and psychological well-being in middle-aged and older Mexican-Americans. Sociological Analysis 49:66-72.

Objective: Examines relationship between church attendance and life-satisfaction among middle-aged and elderly Mexican-Americans. *Sample & Methods*: Random community sample of 375 middle-aged (mean age 49) and 375 elderly Mexican-Americans (mean age 74) from San Antonio, Texas; two-thirds women and most Catholic. Life satisfaction measured using Neugarten Life Satisfaction Index; church attendance assessed with 6-point Likert scale. *Results*: After controlling for a wide range of demographic variables, subjective health, and functional health, church attendance was significantly correlated with life satisfaction in women (middle-aged women, $p < .01$; older women, $p < .05$); church attendance was unrelated to life satisfaction in men. *Conclusions*: Even after controlling for subjective and functional health, church attendance remains a predictor of high life satisfaction in middle-aged and elderly Mexican-American women. *Quality*: Very good.

75. Willits, F.K., and D.M. Crider. 1988. Religion and well-being: Men and women in the middle years. Review of Religious Research 29(3):281-294.

Objective: Examines relationships between adolescent, parent, and adult religiosity measures to overall personal well-being and satisfaction with life. *Sample & Methods*: Panel study of over 1500 Pennsylvania high school students initially surveyed in 1947 and then again in 1984 (1,650 respondents). Parents' church attendance and adolescent religious participation were taken from 1947 survey. At the second survey, most respondents were in their 50's. *Results*: Parents' church attendance was related to respondents' adult church attendance (father $r = .20$, $p < .001$; mother $r = .19$, $p < .001$) and religious beliefs (father $r = .08$, $p < .01$; mother $r = .07$, $p < .05$). Father's church attendance (but not mother's) was significantly related to respondents' adult life satisfaction ($r = .07$, $p < .01$). An interaction with sex was present, with some relationships strongest in women (marital satisfaction) and others strongest in men (job satisfaction). Respondents' adult church attendance and religious belief were significantly related to community, job, and marital satisfaction. *Conclusions*: Parental church attendance (particularly the father's) was significantly related to both adult religiosity and life satisfaction for respondents. Present day church attendance and religious belief were also related to greater satisfaction in multiple domains of life. *Quality*: Very good. A most fascinating and unique study that examines the influence of parent's religious activity on the adult religious activity and life-satisfaction of adolescents.

76. Ellison, C.G., D.A. Gay, and T.A. Glass. 1989. Does religious commitment contribute to individual life satisfaction? Social Forces 68:100-123.
Objective: Authors review the literature and examine their own data to examine the relationship between church attendance and life satisfaction. *Sample & Methods*: Data for this analysis came from the 1983 NORC General Social Survey, a nationally representative sample of adults; paper does not provide a total N or any description of the sample. Life satisfaction, the dependent variable, was measured by 4 variables which were summed. Six multivariate regression models were examined, sequentially adding strength of religious affiliation, frequency of attendance, and devotional intensity to the models. *Results*: A positive relationship was found between attendance and satisfaction that persisted after controlling for non-religious social participation (both intensity and affiliation). *Conclusions*: The relationship between church attendance and life satisfaction cannot be entirely explained in terms of the positive effects of social interaction. *Quality*: Good. This study was included because it confirms other work indicating that the positive mental health effects of frequent church attendance are not due simply to increased socialization.

77. Koenig, H.G., I.C. Siegler, and L.K. George. 1989. Religious and
    non-religious coping: Impact on adaptation. Journal of Religion
    and Aging 5(4):73-94

Objective: Examines the relationship between religious coping and
twelve established social psychological measures of adaptation and
adjustment among older adults. *Sample & Methods*: Stratified random
sample of 100 older participants in the Duke Longitudinal Study of
Aging (II). Subjects were 50% men and 50% women; mean age was
67 years; average educational level was at least some college; 73%
were married and 90% were from a Protestant background. Open
ended questions were asked about how participants coped with the
three event-periods noted above; responses were tape-recorded and
categorized as "religious" or "non-religious." Religious and non-
religious copers were assessed in terms of life satisfaction (Neugarten
and Cantril's scales), negative affect, positive affect, affect balance,
self-esteem, locus of control (Rotter and Jessor scales), trust, anomie,
overall adjustment, and likelihood of giving socially desirable responses.
Results: Despite coming from a lower social class and reporting more
stressful life experiences, religious copers achieved the highest coping
scores on 9 of the 12 coping measures. These differences, however,
did not reach statistical significance. *Conclusions*: For older persons of
lower social class who experience high levels of stress, religious
behaviors (when used frequently) may be associated with high levels
of adaptation.

78. Kvale, J.N., H.G. Koenig, C. Ferrel, & H.R. Moore. 1989. Life
    satisfaction of the aging woman religious. Journal of Religion
    and Aging 5(4):59-71.

Objective: To examine differences in well-being between a sample of
retired elderly nuns, community-dwelling elderly women, and
community-dwelling elderly men. *Sample & Methods*: Convenience
sample of 183 elderly nuns, 439 elderly women, and 191 elderly men
living in the mid-West (Illinois, Iowa, Missouri) completed
questionnaires inquiring about well-being (Philadelphia Geriatric Center
Morale Scale). *Results*: Elderly nuns were less likely to experience
worry that interferes with sleep (p < .0001), less likely to note that
things keep getting worse as they grow older (p < .01), more likely to
agree that things were getting better as they grow older (p < .01), more
likely to agree that "I am as happy now as when I was younger"
(p < .0001), less likely to feel lonelier with age (p < .05), less likely to
agree that sometimes life is not worth living (p < .0001), more likely to
admit that "I am satisfied with my life today" (p < .0001), and less
likely to admit that they have a lot to be sad about (p = .01). *Conclusions*: Elderly retired nuns have relatively high life satisfaction and well-

being, particularly when compared with other elderly women and elderly men living in the community. *Quality*: Good. There are some clinical reports that elderly nuns are more likely to have obsessive-compulsive disorder (personal communication, George Grossberg MD), although there exist no published studies documenting this.

79. Levin, J.S. 1989. Religious factors in aging, adjustment, and health: A theoretical overview. In William M. Clements (Ed), Religion, Aging and Health: A Global Perspective. New York: Haworth Press, pp 133-142

Objective: Dr. Levin, a widely renowned public health expert in the field, reviews and critiques the evidence for a relationship between religious factors and health in later life. *Sample & Methods*: Review and discussion. *Results & Conclusions*: After examining over two dozen gerontological studies that link religiosity to well-being, he concludes that (1) church attendance and involvement exert a positive effect on well-being, and (2) nonorganizational or private religious activities may increase slightly to compensate for the health-related decline in church attendance and communal activity. *Quality*: Very Good.

80. Koenig, H.G., I.C. Siegler, K.G. Meador, and L.K. George. 1990. Religious coping and personality in later life. International Journal of Geriatric Psychiatry 5:123-131.

Objective: Examines the cross-sectional and longitudinal relationship between religious coping and personality in later life. *Sample & Methods*: Stratified random sample of 100 older participants in the Second Duke Longitudinal Study of Aging (DLSA) chosen from the membership roster of the North Carolina Blue Cross-Blue Shield Insurance company. Subjects were 50% men and 50% women; mean age was 67 years; average educational level was at least some college; 73% were married and 90% were from a Protestant background. Open ended questions were asked about how participants coped with the worst event in their lives, the worst event in the past 10 years, and the worse thing about the present; responses were tape-recorded and categorized as "religious" or "non-religious." Personality was measured using the Cattell 16-PF during Wave I and Wave IV of the Second DLSA (1968-1976). *Results*: Religious copers were more likely to score low on Factor E measuring dominance, aggressiveness, and hostility; e.g., they were more likely to be submissive, humble, considerate, and diplomatic (p<.0005). Religious copers were also more likely to score higher on Factor I, indicating greater sensitivity, tender-mindedness, kindness, and gentleness (p<.01). Over a six year interval, women who used religion to cope showed a decline in Factor

Q4, suggesting an increase in relaxation, tranquility, and composure over time, compared with non-religious copers (p < .03). *Conclusions*: Religious coping is both cross-sectionally & longitudinally related to positive personality traits in older adults.

81. O'Connor, B.P., and R.J. Vallerand. 1990. Religious motivation in the elderly: A French-Canadian replication and extension. Journal of Social Psychology 130(1):53-59.
Objective: Examines the relationship between religious motivation and personal adjustment among the elderly. *Sample & Methods*: Four types of religious motivation (intrinsic, self-determined extrinsic, non-self-determined extrinsic, and amotivational) were assessed in a sample of 176 elderly French-Canadians (Quebec) and correlated with personal adjustment. *Results & Conclusions*: Religiosity was related to both better personal adjustment and to other important aspects of these subjects' lives. *Quality*: Good; one of the few studies outside the United States that has addressed this topic.

82. Ellison, C.G. 1991. Religious involvement and subjective well-being. Journal of Health and Social Behavior 32:80-99.
Objective: Examines the complex relationship between religious involvement and well-being. *Sample & Methods*: Data on 948 persons of all ages taken from the 1988 General Social Survey, a national cross-sectional sample of adults in the United States. Life satisfaction was measured by 5-item scale (response range for each item 1-8); personal happiness was measured using a single item (response range 1-3). Four dimensions of religious involvement were assessed: denominational ties, social integration, divine relations, and existential certainty. *Results*: The beneficial effects of church attendance and private devotion were primarily indirect, through their strengthening of religious belief systems. Religious certainty, however, had a direct and substantial influence on well-being. Persons with a stronger faith reported higher life satisfaction, personal happiness, and fewer negative consequences to stressful life events. The relationship with life satisfaction was greater for older than younger adults. *Conclusions*: "Engagement of a divine other in later life may help to compensate for adverse psychosocial consequences associated with the aging process." *Quality*: Very good. Hierarchical OLS regression models used to estimate effects.

83. Morris, D.C. 1991. Church attendance, religious activities, and the life satisfaction of older adults in Middletown, U.S.A. Journal of Religious Gerontology 8(1):83-96.
Objective: Examines the pattern of relationships between church

attendance, religious activity, sex, income, age, health, and subjective well-being. *Sample & Methods*: A random sample of 400 community-dwelling adults age 60 or over located in Middletown, Indiana, were contacted by telephone and surveyed; 67% were women, 53% were married, 57% had an income above $10,000/yr, 62% had at least a high school education, and 44% attended church once/wk or more. Life satisfaction was assessed with a single-item measure (poor, fair, good, excellent). *Results*: The most important predictors of life satisfaction were subjective health status, satisfaction with income, and church attendance (Model R-square = .23). Path analysis is used to demonstrate the direct and indirect effects of these and other variables on life satisfaction. *Conclusions*: Even after controlling for subjective health and satisfaction with income, church attendance remained a significant predictor of life satisfaction (beta = 0.11, p < .05). *Quality*: Good. Study uses path analysis to demonstrate the inter-relationships between sex, education, age, health, financial well-being, church attendance, and life satisfaction.

84. Thomas, L.E. 1991. Dialogues with three religious renunciates and reflection on wisdom and maturity. International Journal of Aging and Human Development 32(3): 211-227.

Objective: Examines life-satisfaction and maturity among elderly Hindus. *Method*: Indepth interviews with 3 elderly male Hindu religious renunciates living in India. Subjects selected by their acquaintances as being spiritually mature. *Results*: Subjects were rated as highly mature using Western developmental standards; Western correlates of life satisfaction, however, were not found to be true for these men. *Conclusions*: Generalizations concerning spiritual maturity and its relationship to life satisfaction must be made carefully in different religious traditions. Results also emphasize the importance of contemplation and acceptance of death. *Quality*: Fair; small sample limits certainty of conclusions. However, this represents one of the few papers that addresses the relationship between spirituality and mental health in a religious tradition outside of Judeo-Christianity.

85. Williams, D.R., D.B. Larson, R.E. Buckler, R.C. Heckman, and C.M. Pyle. 1991. Religion and psychological distress in a community sample. Social Science and Medicine 32:1257-1262.

Objective: Explores the relationship between religious behavior and mental health by examining how religious attendance and religious affiliation combine with stress to affect psychological distress.
Sample & Methods: A longitudinal study of 938 adults first interviewed in 1967 and again in 1969 (n = 720). Participants were from New Haven, Connecticut; mean age was 44.8, 44% male, 11%

Black.   Gurin symptom checklist of psychological distress was the
mental health measure utilized. *Results & Conclusions*: While religious
attendance was not related to psychological well-being when initial
health status was controlled, there was an interaction between religion
and stress such that religious attendance decreased the negative
consequences of stress on psychological well-being (evidence for a
classic stress-buffering effect). *Quality:* Very Good.   Although the
study was not restricted to an elderly sample, the results may be quite
applicable - given the increased levels of stress from loss and health
problems that elders experience.

86.   Holt, M.K., and M. Dellman-Jenkins. 1992.   Research and
      implications for practice: Religion, well-being/morale, and
      coping behavior in later life.   Journal of Applied Gerontology
      11:101-110.
Objective: Seeks to increase gerontology professionals' awareness of
the importance of religion to older adults and of its potential as a
resource for enhancing quality of life. *Method*: Review and discussion.
Results & Conclusions: There is empirical validation for religion's
helpfulness in maintaining morale and well-being in later life.
Implications for clergy and gerontology professionals are discussed in
terms of service provision - emphasizes the need for cooperation and
understanding between mental health, social service, and religious
professionals. *Quality*: Good; an informative review.

87. Utsch, M. 1992. Religiositat im alter: Forschungsschwerpunkte
      und methodische probleme [Religion in aging: Main research
      points and methodologic problems].   Zeitschrift der
      Gerontologie 25(1):25-31.
Objective: To examine and summarize studies exploring the relationship
between mental health and religiosity in older adults (focus on German
studies). *Sample & Methods*: Literature review and discussion. *Results
& Conclusions*: Studies have explored the relationship between religion,
health, coping, and the search for meaning among elderly persons.
Methodological concerns are raised and discussed. *Quality*: Fair.   A
valuable reference for studies examining this topic outside of the
United States.

      Anxiety (community studies)

88.   Morris, P.A.   1982.   The effect of pilgrimage on anxiety,
      depression and religious attitude.   Psychological Medicine
      12:291-294.

Objective: Examines levels of anxiety, depression, and religious attitude in a group of physically ill older adults both prior to and after a pilgrimage to Lourdes. *Sample & Methods*: 24 person (average age 63) with chronic medical illness (46% men) from the Nottingham Catholic Diocese. Religious Attitude Scale, State-Trait Anxiety Inventory, and a Depression Inventory were administered 1 month before the trip, 1 months afterwards, and 10 months afterwards. *Results*: There was a significant lessening of anxiety in both men and women following he visit to Lourdes, that was sustained over the year of followup. Likewise, depression scores decreased significantly after the trip and continued to decline during the next year. *Conclusions*: Older persons with chronic health problems who made a religious pilgrimage to Lourdes showed significant mental health benefits from this experience, including a lessening of both anxiety and depression that lasted for at least 10 months after their return home. *Quality*: Good. The only study I am aware of that documents the mental health effects of a religious pilgrimage.

89.   Koenig, H.G., L.K. George, D.G. Blazer, J. Pritchett, and K.G. Meador. 1993. Journal of Geriatric Psychiatry 26(1):65-93.
Objective: Examines the relationship between religion and anxiety in community-dwelling older adults. *Sample & Methods*: The sample was composed of 1299 persons aged 60 or over participating in Wave II of the Piedmont NIMH Epidemiologic Catchment Area survey. Church attendance, prayer and Bible reading, religious TV viewing, importance of religion, "born again" status, and denominational affiliation were measured. Anxiety symptoms and disorders were assessed using the Diagnostic Interview Schedule using DSM-III criteria. Analyses were cross-sectional and examined relationships between religious variables and both 6-month and lifetimes rates of anxiety disorder. *Results*: Uncontrolled analyses found that anxiety symptoms were lower among frequent church attenders, but higher among those frequently viewing religious TV programs, those considering themselves "born again", and those affiliated with Pentecostal or conservative Protestant affiliations. All these associations lost their significance when control variables were taken into account. For anxiety disorders, 6-month and lifetime rates were higher among those who frequently prayed or read the Bible, and simple phobia was more common in Pentecostals and conservative Protestants; again these differences disappeared when socioeconomic status, sex, chronic illness, and recent life events were controlled for. *Conclusions*: While these data demonstrate no significant independent relationship between religion and anxiety disorder in later life, dynamic factors may effectively mask an underlying association; for example, if older persons turn to religion

when excessively anxious, this could mask a protective or therapeutic effect for religion.

90. Koenig, H.G., S. Ford, L.K. George, D.G. Blazer, and K.G. Meador. 1993. Religion and anxiety disorder: An examination and comparison of association in young, middle-aged, and elderly adults. Journal of Anxiety Disorders 7:321-342.
Objective: Investigators examine the effects of age on the relationship between religion and anxiety disorder. *Sample & Methods*: Data on 1025 young adults (ages 18-39), 645 middle-aged adults (ages 40 to 59), and 1299 elderly adults (ages 60 to 97) from the 1983-84 Piedmont NIMH Epidemiologic Catchment Area survey were examined for associations between religion and anxiety disorder. Religious variables included church attendance, Bible-reading and prayer, importance of religion, "born again" status, and religious affiliation. Anxiety disorders were diagnosed using the Diagnostic Interview Schedule which uses DSM-III criteria; 6-month and lifetime rates of anxiety disorder were examined. All analyses were controlled for sex, chronic illness, negative life events, and SES. *Results*: Associations were strongest among young adults. Rates of anxiety disorder were significantly lower among frequent church attenders, mainline Protestants, and those considering themselves "born again." However, anxiety disorders were significantly more common among Pentecostal affiliates, those with no religious affiliation, and those who frequently watched religious TV. All relationships weakened in middle-aged and older adults. *Conclusions*: There is a complex pattern of both positive and negative relationships between religious factors and anxiety disorder in younger adults; these relationships weaken in later life when dynamic factors become more influential.

Depression (community studies)

91. Morse, C.K. and P.A. Wisocki. 1987. Importance of religiosity to elderly adjustment. Journal of Religion and Aging 4(1):15-27.
Objective: Examines the extent to which religious beliefs and church attendance influence psychological adjustment in later life. *Sample & Methods*: 156 persons over age 60 (mean 72 years) recruited from senior centers in Western Massachusetts; sample composed of 71% women, 49% widowed, 65% with current income less than $10,000/yr, 73% with at least a high school education. Religious items included church membership, attendance, comfort from religion, and extent to which religion provides meaning to life; scores to these

items were summed to form a religiosity index (range 2-10); patients were divided into high and low religious participation by dichotomizing scores at the median. Psychological adjustment was measured by Mood Adjective Checklist, SCL-90, and a Worry Scale. *Results*: On both the SCL-90 and the Mood Adjective Checklist, subjects with high religiosity scores were significantly less likely to be depressed and anxious; they also reported less somatization, phobia, and aggression than did subjects with low religiosity scores. Controlling for number of chronic illnesses weakened the negative association between religiosity and anxiety, but did not affect the inverse relationship with depression which remained significant. *Conclusions*: Elderly people with higher levels of religious activity and beliefs show greater psychological health and adjustment. *Quality*: Good.

92. Rosik, C.H. 1989. The impact of religious orientation in conjugal bereavement among older adults. International Journal of Aging and Human Development 28:251-260.

Objective: Focuses on the relationship between religiosity and adjustment to widowhood. *Sample & Methods*: Grief, depression, and intrinsic-extrinsic religiosity were examined in a sample of 159 elderly widowed persons participating in support groups located in Southern California. Hierarchical regression models were used to examine associations between depression and religiosity measures, controlling for other relevant factors. The Geriatric Depression Scale and Texas Grief Inventory were used to assess emotional distress. The measure of extrinsic religion was heavily weighted in terms of support and comfort received from religion. *Results*: Extrinsic religiosity was positively related to higher distress levels in both males and females. Widowers who were indiscriminately pro-religious also had higher distress levels. Intrinsic religiosity showed no consistent relationship with either depression or grief. *Conclusions*: Extrinsic religiosity may be a risk factor for maladjustment in both sexes after conjugal bereavement, and indiscriminate pro-religiousness may have the same effect in elderly widowers. *Quality*: Good, although author minimizes the possibility that bereaved elders might have turned to religion for support and comfort even before the death of the spouse, thus artificially creating a positive association between religiousness and grief or depression.

93. Kennedy, G., W. Wisniewski, H. Kelman, C. Thomas, and H. Metz. 1990. Religious preference, attendance at services and the prevalence of depressive symptoms in the elderly. The Gerontologist 30:260A.

Objective: Examines and compares the prevalence of depressive symptoms among elderly Jews and Catholics. *Sample & Methods*: Urban sample of community-dwelling elderly persons in New York (n = 2129). Sample composed of 39% Jews and 48% Catholic. Jews were on the average 2.3 years older than Catholics, had 1.4 more years of education, and had more physical health problems. CES-D was used to measure depressive symptoms. *Results & Conclusions*: Symptoms of depression were significantly more common among Jews (24%) than Catholics (12%). Attendance at religious services was significantly less common among Jews than Catholics. Holocaust survivorship was significantly related to depressive symptoms among Jews, but not Catholics. *Quality*: Good. Greater physical health problems could at least partly explain the higher rate of depressive symptoms in Jews.

94. Nelson, P.B. 1990. Religious orientation of the elderly. Journal of Gerontological Nursing 16(2):29-35.

Objective: Examines the relationship between intrinsic/extrinsic religious orientation, depression, and self-esteem among older adults. *Sample & Methods*: Data was gathered from a convenience sample of 68 community-dwelling adults aged 55 or over participating in an elderly day care program in Austin, Texas; sample composed of 47% White, 50% Black, and 3% Mexican-Americans; 78% of the sample were women and 46% of the sample was widowed. Intrinsic and extrinsic religious orientation was assessed with the Age Universal Religious Orientation Scale (alternate form of Allport and Ross' scale), depression was assessed with the Geriatric Depression Scale, and self-esteem with the Rosenberg Self-Esteem Scale. *Results*: Intrinsic religious orientation was inversely related to both depression ($r = -.23$, $p < .05$) and low self-esteem ($r = -.38$, $p = .001$); extrinsic religiosity was related to neither depression or self-esteem. *Conclusions*: Religion is a source of support in the lives of the elderly; implications for nursing care are discussed. *Quality*: Fair.

95. Goodman, M., R.L. Rubinstein, B.B. Alexander, and M. Luborsky. 1991. Cultural differences among elderly women in coping with the death of an adult child. Journal of Gerontology 46:S321-S329.

Objective: Researchers at the Philadelphia Geriatric Center explore differences between elderly Jewish and non-Jewish women in their ability to cope with the death of an adult child. *Sample & Methods*: Interviews obtained from 12 Jewish and 17 non-Jewish women participating in a larger study examining well-being in elderly women; indepth life histories were gathered, along with quantitative assessments of well-being, affect, generativity, and personality.

Results & Conclusions: Compared with non-Jewish women, Jewish women were on the average more depressed and struggling with unresolved grief, which continued to play a central position in their lives. Non-Jewish women were more likely to express philosophies of acceptance and moving on with their lives. Quantitative measures of well-being, affect, and personality statistically supported these qualitative differences between Jewish and non-Jewish women. *Quality*: Very Good.

96. Meador, K.G., H.G. Koenig, J. Turnbull, D.G. Blazer, L.K. George, and D. Hughes. 1992. Religious affiliation and depression. Hospital & Community Psychiatry 43:1204-1208.
Objective: Examines the relationship between religious affiliation and major depression. *Sample & Methods*: Data on 2,850 adults participating in NIMH Epidemiologic Catchment Area survey (Piedmont, North Carolina site) were examined the determine the association between major depression (Diagnostic Interview Schedule using DSM-III criteria) and religious affiliation. A logistic regression analysis was used to control for gender, age, race, SES, negative life events, and social support. *Results*: Pentecostal affiliates were three times as likely to experience a major depression within the past 6 months as non-Pentecostal affiliates (OR 3.1, 95% CI 1.2-8.1, p<.05). Most of the cases of depression were found among younger women, and this relationship weakened with age. *Conclusions*: Pentecostal religious affiliation is associated with higher rates of major depression, especially among younger adults. This relationship weakens in later life. *Quality*: Very good.

97. Koenig, H.G. 1994. Religious affiliation and psychiatric disorder among Protestant baby boomers. Hospital & Community Psychiatry 45:586-596.
Objective: Examines the association between psychiatric disorders and religious affiliation among community-dwelling adults born between 1945 and 1966 (baby boomers), and compares these results to those in mid-life and old age. *Sample & Methods*: The participants in the study were a random sample of community-dwelling adults surveyed during the 1983-84 Epidemiologic Catchment Area study at the Piedmont, North Carolina site. The sample was composed of 853 Protestant baby boomers (aged 18 to 39) and 1,826 Protestants in middle or older age (40 to 59 and 60 or over). *Results*: Pentecostal baby boomers were found to have significantly higher 6-month and lifetime rates of depressive disorder, anxiety disorder, and any DSM-III disorder. Mainline Protestants had the lowest 6-month rates of any DSM-III disorder. These relationships weakened in middle-aged and

older adults, although a new relationship emerged with alcohol abuse-dependence; older Pentecostals had significantly higher recent and life-time rates of alcohol abuse-dependence than did old adults affiliated with conservative Protestant or Mainline Protestant traditions. When analyses were stratified by church attendance, it was discovered that most of the increased rates of psychiatric disorder among Pentecostals was due to high rates of disorder among infrequent church attenders. It was also discovered that despite high rates of recent psychiatric problems in the latter group, not a single person had seen a mental health professional in the past 6 months. *Conclusions*: Infrequent church attenders associated with Pentecostal denominations are at high risk for psychiatric disorder, and seldom seek professional help for these problems. *Note*: Important to read the discussion of this paper to understand the implications of the findings.

98. Ellison C.G. 1995. Race, religious involvement, and depressive symptomatology in a southeastern U.S. community. Social Science and Medicine, in press.
Objective: Examines the relationship between religious involvement and depressive symptoms, comparing results in Whites and Blacks. *Sample & Methods*: Random sample of 2,956 community-dwelling adults involved in Wave II of the Piedmont Health Survey (North Carolina), one of five sites of the National Institute of Mental Health Epidemiologic Catchment Area Program. Dependent variable was "total number of Diagnostic Interview Schedule depressive symptoms [experienced within the past 6 months] not explained by physical illness, injury or drug use." Religious variables included church attendance, private religious devotions (prayer or Bible study), and religious affiliation (present or absent). Hierarchical regression models were used to examine these cross-sectional relationships. *Results*: Church attendance was inversely related to depressive symptoms among Whites (B=-.04, p<.01), but not Blacks (B= +.03, p=ns). Religious devotional activity was positively related to depressive symptoms in both Whites (B= +.05, p<.001) and Blacks (B= +.06, p<.001). Absence of religious affiliation was strongly related to depressive symptoms in Blacks (B= +.58, p<.001), but not in Whites (B= +.02, p=ns). *Conclusions*: Depressive symptoms appear to be differentially related to different aspects of religious involvement in Blacks and Whites. *Quality*: Very good. Persons invariably "turn to" personal religion during a time of crisis or emotional turmoil - like depression. Thus, a positive relationship between depression and private activities like prayer and Bible reading would be expected. Church attendance may be a more stable indicator of religious involvement. On the other hand, depression may have a greater impact on church attendance in

Whites than in Blacks; in other words, Blacks may continue to go to church even when they are feeling bad and depressed, whereas Whites more quickly reduce church attendance (giving rise to an inverse relationship between depressive symptoms and church attendance).

Black Elderly

99. Ortega, S.T., R.D. Crutchfield, and W.A. Rushing. 1983. Race differences in elderly personal well-being: Friendship, family and church. Research on Aging 5:101-108.

Objective: Examines the relationship between well-being, support from family, and support from church friends. Sample & Methods: A random sample of households in urban, rural and isolated rural areas of a northern Alabama county, yielding a total of 4522 adults age 18 or older; patients over age 65 (n = 689) were the focus of this analysis. Three single item measures of "happiness", general life satisfaction", and "relative life satisfaction" were used. *Results:* An association between race (Blacks) and life satisfaction was found in the elderly; this relationship was due, at least in part, to greater contact with church-related friends among the Black elderly. A high frequency of contact with church friends was associated with higher well-being, whereas frequent contacts with family members or non-church related friends was not. *Conclusions*: Among older members in this sample, frequent contacts with church friends was more strongly related well-being than contacts with either non-church friends or with relatives. *Quality*: Good. This study emphasizes the important role that the church plays in providing high quality social support for older adults; the higher life satisfaction in older Blacks (compared with Whites) was largely attributed to their frequent contact with church friends.

100. Farakahan, A., and W.A. O'Connor. 1984. Life satisfaction and depression among retired Black persons. Psychological Reports 55:452-454.

Objective: Examine the correlates of life satisfaction among elderly Black persons before retirement, immediately after retirement, and one month thereafter. *Sample & Methods*: Convenience sample of 30 elderly Blacks (77% women) ages 52-97 years (mean 71) from rural areas in Missouri. Life satisfaction assessed with the Ecosystem Assessment Record and Depression Adjective Checklist. *Results*: From pre-retirement to post-retirement, elderly Blacks decreased their overall activities, but increased time spent with family and increased church attendance and participation in religiously oriented activities. Primary correlates of life satisfaction were health, family, church, and private or intimate time spent. *Conclusions*: After retirement, the church and family take increasing importance for elderly Blacks. *Quality*: Fair.

101. Taylor, R.J., and L.M. Chatters. 1988. Church members as a source of informal social support. Review of Religious Research 30:193-203.

Objective: Examines sociodemographic and religious factors as predictors of informal social support received by Black Americans. *Sample & Methods*: 2,107 adults participating in the National Survey of Black Americans conducted in 1979-1980; 41% of sample aged 18-35 yrs, 32% aged 35-54 yrs, 28% over age 55; 62% women; 44% with less than a high school diploma; 51% with incomes less than $10,000; and 42% married or common law. Dependent variables were "probability of receiving support" and "probability of never needing vs. never receiving support." *Results*: Nearly two-thirds (64%) of respondents indicated that church members provided some level of support to them: 25% indicated receiving assistance from church members often, 27% sometimes, 12% hardly ever, and 18% never. Support was related to church membership, frequency of attendance, high subjective religiosity, and Baptist affiliation; men were more likely to receive support than women, and married persons more often than divorced persons; and older adults were less likely to receive support than younger persons. Respondents who attend church frequently were more likely to never need support (vs. never receive support); persons with higher incomes and those residing in rural areas were more likely than others to never need assistance from church members. *Conclusions*: Church members are a vital source of assistance to many Black Americans; religion and the church play an important role in the material and psychological support that Black Americans receive. *Quality*: Very good. Also see: Lincoln, C.E., and L.H. Mamiya. 1990. The Black Church in the African American Experience. Durham, NC: Duke University Press [uses both anecdotal and empirical evidence to argue for the central role that religion plays in the lives of Black Americans - not only in promoting well-being, but also playing an instrumental role in the development of Black communities].

102. Handal, P.J., W. Black-Lopez, S. Moergen. 1989. Preliminary investigation of the relationship between religion and psychological distress in Black women. Psychological Reports 65:971-975.

Objective: Investigates the relationship between religion and mental distress among a population of Black women. *Sample & Methods*: Convenience sample of 115 Black women living in the St. Louis metropolitan area; age range was 18 to 67 years; Baptists (38%) and

Catholics (25%) made up the greatest proportion of subjects. Religiosity measured using the Integration subscale of the Personal Religiosity Inventory; high, medium, and low scoring groups were created for analysis. Psychological maladjustment was assessed by the 22-item Langner Symptom Survey. *Results*: Women scoring low on religious Integration had the highest psychological distress scores compared with either middle or high scoring groups (5.0 vs 2.7 and 3.1, $F = 4.7$, $p < .01$). *Conclusions*: There is a strong association between low religious integration and mental distress. *Quality*: Fair. Black women have seldom been studied as a group in themselves, and these results are both interesting and relevant to older Black women.

103. Krause, N., and T. Van Tran. 1989.   Stress and religious involvement among older Blacks.   Journal of Gerontology 44:S4-S13.

Objective: Explores whether religious involvement helps to reduce the negative impact of stressful life events in older Blacks. *Sample & Methods*: Persons aged 55 or older (n = 511) were selected from a nationwide survey of Black Americans conducted in 1979-1980 (National Survey of Black Americans); older women made up 63% of the sample and 40% of participants were married. Examined were self-esteem, mastery, stressful life events, and religious involvement (church membership, church attendance, importance of church, frequency of prayer, importance of religious services for children, and self-rated religiosity). Three different interactive models (suppressor, moderator, distress-deterrent) were assessed by structural equation modeling (LISREL). *Results*: Stress and religious involvement exerted direct additive effects on mastery and self-esteem; however, there was no relationship between stress and religiosity, and the impact of stress on self-esteem and mastery was not contingent upon the level of current religiosity. *Conclusions*: Support was found only for a distress-deterrent model; in other words, while life stress tended to diminish feelings of self-worth and mastery, increased religious involvement appeared to offset or counterbalance this effect. *Quality*: Excellent; among the most methodologically sophisticated of studies done to date.

104. Ellison, C.G., and D.A. Gay. 1990. Region, religious commitment, and life satisfaction among Black Americans. The Sociological Quarterly 31:123-147.

Objective: Examines relationship between religious commitment and life-satisfaction in Blacks, considering both age and regional effects. *Sample & Methods*: Used data from the National Survey of Black Americans conducted by University of Michigan Survey Research

Center in 1979-1980. This is a nationally representative sample of 2,107 Black adults; the sample is slightly older and more female, and residents of western states are under-represented when compared with US Census Bureau data. A series of hierarchical regression models is presented, with religious variables entered sequentially after control variables have been entered. Analyses were stratified by "southern" and "non-southern" regions. *Results:* Only in the non-southern subsample did a significant relationship arise between life satisfaction and both religious participation and religiosity; these relationships were strongest among older Blacks. All analyses were controlled for health and a wide variety of psychosocial variables, including social support (social network size, degree of social interaction, and perception of closeness of family). *Conclusions:* First, these findings demonstrate a relationship between religion and well-being in non-southern states (outside of the Bible Belt). Second, they demonstrate a stronger relationship between life satisfaction and religiosity among elderly Blacks than younger Blacks. Third, they suggest that the impact of church attendance and communal religious involvement on life satisfaction reflects something more than simply the positive effects of social support and health. *Quality:* Very Good.

105. Walls, C.T., and S.H. Zarit. 1991. Informal support from Black churches and the well-being of elderly Blacks. Gerontologist 31:490-495.

Objective: Examines the amount and type of support received by elders from Black churches and from their families, and its relationship to well-being. *Sample & Methods:* 98 Black adults aged 65 to 104, recruited from local Black churches located in an urban area in Pennsylvania, were interviewed to assess perceptions of support from either church or family; 75% of the sample were women, 40% were married and 53% widowed; they had an average 10 yrs education and median income of $9,000/yr. Social network was assessed and correlations with well-being determined. *Results:* 40% of important or close people in their networks were from the church, 50% from their family. Family rated higher on all six measures of perceived support. Neither the spiritual aspect of religiosity nor involvement in organized religious activities predicted well-being, although perceived overall support from church members did predicted well-being ($F = 4.4$, $p < .05$). *Conclusions:* The family network was perceived as more supportive than the church network, although the latter contributed to feelings of well-being. *Quality:* Good; one of few studies that did not find a strong association between well-being and religiosity or religious involvement in older Blacks.

106. Coke, M.M. 1992. Correlates of life satisfaction among elderly
       African Americans. Journal of Gerontology 47:P316-P320.
Objective: Examines correlates of life satisfaction among older Black
Americans. *Sample & Methods*: Surveyed 166 community-dwelling
(New York) Black adults aged 65 to 88 years; regression analyses were
run separately for males (n=87) and females (n=79). *Results*:
Females had both higher life satisfaction and higher church
participation than males. Among males, hours of church participation,
subjective religiosity, family role involvement, self-perceived adequacy
of income, actual income, and years of education, were all related to
higher life satisfaction. Among females, only self-rated religiosity was
a significant predictor of life satisfaction. *Conclusions*: Subjective
religiosity, participation in church activities, and family role involvement
were significant predictors of life satisfaction in this population; sex
differences were notable. *Quality*: Good.

107. Krause, N. 1992. Stress, religiosity, and psychological well-being
       among older Blacks. Journal of Aging and Health 4:412-439.
Objective: Tests the theory that religiosity (church attendance and
subjective importance) is an important coping resource for elderly
Blacks. *Sample & Methods*: Data extracted from a national probability
sample of 448 Blacks aged 60 years or over surveyed by the University
of Michigan Survey Research Center in 1986 (Americans' Changing
Lives Survey); average age was 70 years, average education was 8.6
years, and 63% of sample were women. Used structural equation
modeling (LISREL 7) to assess relationships between (1) family deaths
and health problems (stressors), (2) religiosity, (3) receipt of emotional
support, and (4) sense of personal control, self-esteem, and depressed
affect (outcome variables). *Results*: Religiosity tended to
counterbalance or offset the deleterious effects of physical health
problems and deaths (stressors) by bolstering feelings of self-worth;
this effect of religiosity was independent of the level of informal
emotional support that subjects received. *Conclusions*: Religiosity is
an important coping resource for older Blacks; religious commitment
affects psychological well-being independent of the effects of social
support. *Quality*: Excellent; among the methodologically most
sophisticated studies done to date.

108. Nye, W.P. 1992-93. Amazing grace: Religion and continuity
       among elderly Black individuals. International Journal of Aging
       and Human Development 36(2):103-114.
Objective: Examines the role that religion plays in maintaining
continuity in the lives of elderly Blacks. *Sample & Methods*: The
sample consisted of 43 African Americans aged 56-94 years who

resided in southwestern Virginia. Data were studied using content analysis of audiotaped "life stories". *Results & Conclusions*: Religion served at least 7 functions in the normal aging process of these elderly subjects that contributed to their maintaining continuity and stability in their lives. *Quality*: Good, although small sample and potentially biased given location where subjects were drawn from.

109. Levin, J.S., L.M. Chatters, and R.J. Taylor. 1995. Religious effects on health status and life satisfaction among Black Americans. Journal of Gerontology (social sciences), in press.
Objective: Tests a theoretical model linking religion, health and life satisfaction. *Sample & Methods*: Participants were a nationally representative cross-sectional sample of 1848 Black Americans (60% response rate) (National Survey of Black Americans). The sample had a mean age of 42 years, tended to be urban (79%), female (62%), and had a low annual family income (mean $8500). Using a sophisticated statistical technique, covariance-structure-modeling (LISREL 7), these investigators examined relationships between religious variables, health and life satisfaction. *Results*: Older age, female sex, and geographic location (South and rural) were all related to higher religiosity. Organizational religiosity (church attendance, etc.) was significantly related to both better health and higher life satisfaction; non-organizational religiosity (prayer, reading religious literature, etc.) was related to poorer health, but not lower life satisfaction; and subjective religiosity was related only to higher life satisfaction. The relationship between organizational religiosity and life satisfaction persisted even after health status was controlled. *Conclusions*: The association between religion and well-being was substantiated, and could not simply be explained by confounding between church attendance and health. In fact, organizational religiosity was at least as important to well-being as was physical health. Their model fitted equally well in young (age < 30 years), middle aged (31 to 54 years), and elderly (>55 years) subjects. *Quality*: Excellent. Among the most methodologically advanced studies to date on this subject.

Muslims

110. Shams, M., and P.R. Jackson. 1993. Religiosity as a predictor of well-being and moderator of the psychological impact of unemployment. Journal of Medical Psychology 66:341-352.
Objective: Examines the impact of relgiosity on the relationship between unemployment and well-being in a Muslim sample. *Sample & Methods*: 139 employed and unemployed male British Asians (all

Muslims) in Sheffield (northern England) were interviewed; 47% were young (ages 18-30) and 53% were middle-aged (ages 31-55). Psychological well-being was measured using the General Health Questionnaire (Goldberg). Religiosity was measured using a religiosity subscale of the Allport-Vernon Scale of Values [Allport, G.W., P.E. Vernon, and G. Lindzey. 1968. Study of Values, 3rd ed. Boston: Houghton Mifflin]. *Results*: Religiosity was significantly higher among middle-aged than younger men (F = 10.32, p < .001). Both a direct effect for religiosity (F = 6.6, p < .01) on well-being and an interaction with employment status (F = 16.7, p < .01) on well-being were discovered. Religiosity was significantly more likely to be related to well-being in the unemployed group (r = .37, p < .001) than in the employed group (r = -.09, p = ns). *Conclusions*: Religiosity, based on a Muslim faith, was significantly related to well-being among a group of unemployed British Asians. This was not true for the employed group. *Quality*: Very good. While not focusing on the elderly, one of the few studies examining the effects of Muslim faith on psychological status. Also, addresses issues related to measurement of religiosity in samples outside of the Judeo-Christian tradition.

111.   Azhart, M.A., S.L. Varma, and A.S. Dharap. 1994. Religious psychotherapy in anxiety disorder patients. Acta Psychiatrica Scandinavica 90:1-3.

Objective: Assesses the effectiveness of religious psychotherapy in the treatment of Muslim patients with anxiety disorder. *Sample & Methods*: All patients attending a psychotherapy clinic in Malaysia were evaluated using a religious questionnaire consisting of 23 questions (rated 1-10 scale) on the patient's beliefs in God, the Holy Koran and the Prophet [English version available on request - contact M.Z. Azhar, School of Medical Sciences, Hospital Universiti Sains Malaysia, 16150 Kubang Kerian, Malaysia]. Seventy-seven patients fulfilled DSM-III-R criteria for generalized anxiety disorder AND scored 5 or higher on 70% or more of the 23 questions, thus fulfilling religious criteria for possible inclusion in the study. Fifteen patients did not complete the full duration of therapy and were dropped. Sixty-two patients were randomly assigned to study or control groups (31 in each group); average age of patients in the study and control groups were 40 and 39 years, respectively. Both groups were started on benzodiazepines for a maximum of 8 weeks. Both groups were given 12-16 weekly supportive psychotherapy for anxiety. Patients in the study group were given additional religious psychotherapy involving having patients read verses from the Holy Koran and encouraging prayer. *Results*: At 3 months, patients in the study group scored significantly lower on the Hamilton Anxiety Rating scale (rated by a psychiatrist blinded to group assignment) (3.8 vs 6.9, t=4.23, p<.001); by 6 months, however, there was no difference between study and control groups. *Conclusions*: Patients given religious psychotherapy responded more rapidly than did those given conventional supportive therapy and drug treatment. *Quality*: Good. A most interesting study - one that could be used as a model for similar studies in older adults examining religion's effect.

Medically III and Disabled

112. Guy, R.F. 1982. Religion, physical disabilities, and life satisfaction in older age cohorts. International Journal of Aging and Human Development 15:225-232.
Objective: Explores the relationship between church attendance, life satisfaction, and age, and examines how increasing physical disability might affect this relationship. *Sample & Methods*: 1,170 community-dwelling adults age 60 or over located in and around Memphis, Tennessee, were sampled using a quota technique; 73% of the final sample were female; 33% were Black; most respondents had less than a high school education. Interviewers administered to each respondent a one-hundred question survey, including Neugarten's Life Satisfaction Index; church attendance was categorized into six levels from "never" to "more than once a week". *Results*: Life satisfaction was significantly related to both current church attendance (p<.001) and church attendance 15 years previously (p<.001). Church attendance decreased with increasing age - but not because of disengagement or loss of interest, but rather because of increasing physical disability. Disabled persons who were unable to attend church but maintained contact via church newsletters, telephone calls, personal or ministerial visits, tended to have higher life satisfaction. *Conclusions*: Church attendance is an important factor in maintaining life satisfaction among many older adults; only when physical disability becomes marked, does attendance decline. *Quality*: Good, although the church attendance-life satisfaction relationship was not controlled for level of physical disability.

113. O'Brien, M.E. 1982. Religious faith and adjustment to long-term hemodialysis. Journal of Religion and Health 21:68-80.
Objective: Examines the relationship between religious faith and adjustment among patients with end-stage renal disease on chronic maintenance hemodialysis. *Sample & Methods*: Purposive sample of 126 chronic hemodialysis patients, aged 21 to 75, chosen from three large metropolitan hemodialysis centers in Washington DC; patients had

to be on dialysis at least 6 months and have no major medical or psychiatric complications. Patients were assessed initially and then again three years later; 63 of the original 126 patients were reassessed. Sample was equally divided between men and women; 75% were Black. *Results*: At baseline, frequency of church attendance and greater perceived importance of religion were related to higher interactional behavior scores, lower alienation scores, and higher compliance with dialysis treatment. Almost three-quarters of the sample indicated that religious or ethical beliefs were to some extent related to the acceptance of their disease and its treatment. On followup, qualitative analysis indicated that 27% of patients reported that the importance of religious faith in adjusting to illness had either changed from negative to positive or had increased significantly during the past 3 years; only 1 respondent changed from positive to negative; and 70% reported no change. *Conclusions*: Religion has a notable impact on long-term adjustment to end-stage renal failure and its treatment. *Quality*: Good.

114. Rosenstiel, A.K., and F.J. Keefe. 1983. The use of coping strategies in chronic low back pain patients: Relationship to patients characteristics and current adjustment. Pain 17:33-44
Objective: Examines the effectiveness of cognitive and behavioral coping strategies used by patients to deal with chronic pain; includes "diverting attention or praying" as one of the strategies. *Sample & Methods*: Sample consisted of 61 chronic low back pain outpatients at Duke University Medical Center referred for behavioral treatment; mean age was 43 years, duration of pain was 6 years, and duration of continuous pain was almost 2 years. Coping Strategy Questionnaire was used to assess three major coping behaviors: cognitive coping and suppression, helplessness, and diverting attention and praying. Outcomes were average level of pain, depression, anxiety, and functional impairment. *Results*: Patients who used diverting attention and praying experienced the highest level of pain and lowest level of functioning; there was no difference in terms of depression level or anxiety. *Conclusions*: In this study, patients high on diverting attention and praying had more pain and functional impairment. *Quality*: Very good. Again, one wonders whether those who were more impaired and in greater pain were more likely to turn to prayer for possible relief; prayer or hoping was the most common coping behavior used in this setting.

115. Spiegel, D., J.R. Bloom, and E. Gottheil. 1983. Family environment as a predictor of adjustment to metastatic breast cancer. Psychosocial Oncology 1(1):33-44.

Objective: Studies the effects of family environment on psychosocial adjustment of women with metastatic breast cancer. *Sample & Methods*: A consecutive series of 109 women with metastatic breast cancer were referred by their oncologists to the study over a 6 month period; 86 completed the first questionnaire, 5 died, and 18 refused. Fifty of the 86 participants were randomly assigned to a weekly support group that focused on helping patients cope with their terminal illness; the other 36 to a control group. 14 women in the treatment group were too ill to participate; 12 women were lost from the control group. Final sample consisted of 54 women; their mean age was 55 years, 62% were married, 9% lived alone, and mean time since diagnosis was 25 months. Family Environment Scale, Family Checklist, Profile of Mood States, and 22-item Belief Systems scale were administered at baseline, four, eight, and twelve months. *Results*: Patients who at baseline reported their families were high in expressiveness, low in conflict, and low in moral-religious orientation tended to show less mood disturbance during the 12 month study period. *Conclusions*: A family atmosphere which encouraged open discussion of feelings and problems, minimized conflict, and de-emphasized religious orientation predicted better mood during the one year of followup; emphasized that "conspiracies of silence" could have an adverse effect on coping and adjustment. *Quality*: Very good. Authors admit that "selection processes" could account for this data, and that patients who turned to religion may have been more stressed out or desperate about their situations. While not strictly dealing with geriatric patients, this study may be applicable to that population.

116. Decker, S.D. and R. Schulz. 1985. Correlates of life satisfaction and depression in middle-aged and elderly spinal cord-injured persons. <u>American Journal of Occupational Therapy</u> 39:740-745.

Objective: Explores factors that relate to the well-being of middle-aged and elderly spinal cord-injured patients. *Sample & Methods*: Convenience sample of 100 patients aged 40 to 73 years with paraplegia or quadriplegia of at least 5 years duration (Pacific Northwest); 90% were male and all were Caucasian. Health, social support, perceived control, life satisfaction (Neugarten Life Satisfaction Index-A), and depression (CES-D) were measured using standardized scales. Religiousness was also measured, although how is not mentioned. *Results*: The strongest correlates of depression were level of perceived control, social support, and perceived health. "Although correlations were low, people who had higher incomes and were more religious also tended to report greater well-being." *Conclusions*: Religiousness, along with a high level of perceived control, social support, and perceived health, contributes to well-being in this population. *Quality*: Good. Religiousness may also have contributed indirectly to well-being by providing a source of perceived control (through God) and increasing social support (through church members), as well as affected perceptions of health and disability. Also see Idler 1987 below (ref 119).

117. Wright, S.D., C.C. Pratt, and V.L. Schmall. 1985. Spiritual support for caregivers of dementia patients. Journal of Religion and Health 24 (Spring): 31-38.

Objective: Examines the role that religious and spiritual factors play in enabling caregivers of dementia patients to maintain personal well-being. *Sample & Methods*: The sample was composed of 240 caregivers. Questionnaires were distributed at educational seminars on Alzheimer's disease and at support group meetings for Alzheimer's caregivers. Questionnaire included a Caregiver Burden Scale, a Family Coping Strategies instrument, and a measure of "spiritual support" as a coping strategy (seek advice from clergy, attend church services, participate in church activities, and faith in God). *Results*: Caregiver burden was positively correlated with passivity, but inversely related to confidence in problem solving, reframing of problems, and presence of extended family. It was also inversely related to spiritual support ($r = -.25$, $p < .01$). Spiritual support, in turn, was significantly correlated with reframing ("the caregiver's ability to redefine a demanding situation in a more acceptable way in order to make the situation more manageable") ($r = .41$, $p < .001$). *Conclusions*: Caregivers with high levels of spiritual support experienced a greater sense of well-being and life satisfaction than did those without spiritual resources. *Quality*: Good. An important topic needing further study. Caregiver well-being is one of the primary determinants of nursing home placement of demented elders.

118. Reed, P.G. 1986. Religiousness among terminally ill and healthy adults. Research in Nursing & Health 9:35-41

Objective: Compares terminally ill with health adults, examining differences in religiousness and sense of well-being. *Sample & Methods*: A purposive sample of 57 terminally ill adults (mean age 55) and 57 healthy adults from Tucson, Arizona, were matched on age, gender, education, and religious affiliation. All participants completed a Religious Perspective Scale (adapted from King and Hunt's Dimensions of Religiosity scales) and an Index of Well-Being (developed by Campbell, Converse, and Rodgers to measure current life satisfaction). *Results*: The terminally ill group scored significantly higher on the religiousness scale than the healthy group (4.1 vs 3.4, p < .001); religiousness was related to gender (female (r = .47, p < .001) in the terminally ill group, but not the healthy group. Well-being was equivalent in both the terminally ill group and the healthy group (10.1 vs 10.0, p = ns). There was a significant relationship between well-being and religiousness in the healthy group (r = .43, p < .001), but not in the terminally ill group (r = .14, p = ns). *Conclusions*: Terminally ill women of middle and older adulthood may experience a heightened religious awareness during the dying experience; the relationship between religiousness and well-being in this group, while in the expected direction, is a complex one. *Quality*: Very good. One of the few studies examining religiousness and well-being in the terminally ill. Note again that turning to religion in the face of death and lack of hope, may have confounded this relationship.

119.   Idler, E.L. 1987. Religious involvement and the health of the elderly: Some hypotheses and an initial test. Social Forces 66:226-238.
Objective: Examines patterns of religious involvement, chronic medical conditions, functional disability and depression among a large community sample of older adults; places a special focus on (1) the interaction between comfort derived from religion (religious coping) and physical illness (number of chronic medical conditions) on functional disability and (2) the interaction between religious importance and functional disability on depression status. *Sample & Methods*: A cross-sectional analysis of data collected on 2811 non-institutionalized elderly residents (41% men) of New Haven, Connecticut, in 1982 as part of the Yale Health and Aging project. *Results*: After controlling for demographic variables and chronic medical conditions, frequent church attendance was associated with lower levels of functional disability and fewer depressive symptoms; note that the association was lessened, but not neutralized, when chronic medical conditions were controlled for. Among men, religious coping modified the association between health conditions and disability; with increasing levels of religious coping, the association between number of chronic medical conditions and disability lessened. Likewise, importance of religion modified the association between disability and depression; with increasing levels of religiousness, the association between disability and depression lessened. To a lesser degree, this was also true for elderly women; at any given level of chronic conditions, the more a woman attended religious services and knew other members of the congregation, the less physically disabled or depressed she was. *Conclusions*: Religious involvement - both personal religiosity (for men) and public religious involvement (for women) - may buffer the impact of (1) chronic medical conditions on inducing physical disability and (2) the impact of

disability on inducing depression. *Quality*: Very good; although at times the discussion extends somewhat beyond the data. Also see Idler and Kasl 1992 below (ref 128).

120. Jenkins, R.A., and K.I. Pargament. 1988. Cognitive appraisals in cancer patients. Social Sciences in Medicine 26:625-633.
Objective: To examine the role of cognitive appraisals in adjustment to cancer. *Sample & Methods*: Sixty-two cancer patients (mean age 56 years, 95% white, 65% female) were drawn from two outpatient chemotherapy clinics in Bloomington, Indiana. Predictors of adjustment included the following: life threat, perceived control over cancer (including God control), coping comparisons, and perceived control over emotional reactions; adjustment was measured by the Rosenberg self-esteem scale, Millon behavioral health inventory, and behavioral upset in medical patients (BUMP) scale (nurses' ratings of patients' adjustment). *Results*: God appraisals correlated positively with self-esteem $(r = 0.25, p < .05)$ and negatively with observed behavioral upset (BUMP) $(r = -0.23, p < .05)$. *Conclusions*: Patients who perceive that God is in control of their cancer have greater self-esteem and experience less behavioral upset than patients without such beliefs. *Quality*: Very Good. A well-designed study conducted by known experts in the area of cognitive appraisal and coping.

121. Kaczorowski, J.M. 1989. Spiritual well-being and anxiety in adults diagnosed with cancer. Hospice Journal 5 (3/4): 105-116.
Objective: Explores relationship between anxiety and spiritual well-being in cancer patients. *Sample & Methods*: Non-random sample of 114 adults (mean age 58) with cancer, primarily breast (38%) and colorectal cancer (19%). Spiritual well-being measured using Ellison & Polouzian's instrument that assesses both religious and existential well-being. State-Trait Anxiety Inventory (Spielberger) used to assess anxiety. *Results*: Spiritual well-being was inversely related to anxiety $(r = -.44, p = .001)$; the relationship was particularly strong among men. The relationship between anxiety and the existential well-being subscale was stronger than with the religious well-being subscale. *Conclusions*: Anxiety is less among cancer patients with high spiritual well-being. *Quality*: Fair. Note that this particular measure of spiritual well-being is contaminated by indicators of well-being in the existential subscale; thus, one would apriori expect a strong inverse correlation between anxiety and the existential subscale.

122. Nelson, P.B. 1989. Social support, self-esteem, and depression in the institutionalized elderly. Issues in Mental Health Nursing

10:55-68.
Objective: Investigates the relationships among depression, social support, self-esteem, and religious participation among nursing home patients. *Sample & Methods*: Convenience sample of 26 patients without prior depression selected from a nursing home and a retirement home in a southwestern city (Austin, Texas); 77% were female and average age was 81 years. Social support was measured using the Norbeck Social Support Questionnaire, self-esteem by the Rosenberg scale, and depression by the Geriatric Depression Scale. *Results*: Relatives made up 47% of the support network, followed by friends 36%, health care providers (8%), and minister (5%). Almost 70% of respondents reported regular participation in religious activity. There was a correlation between religious participation and low depression score (GDS) was r = .39, p < .05). *Conclusions*: Subjects who frequently participated in religious activity were less depressed than those who did not; the direction of effect could not be determined. *Quality*: Good; small sample, but important population about which little is known concerning the relationship between religion and well-being. Also see: Gubrium, J.F. 1993. Speaking of Life. New York: Aldine De Gruyter [indepth interviews with elders that reveal important insights into the way spirituality functions to promote hopefulness amidst the daily trials of life in a nursing home].

123. Keilman, L.J., and B.A. Given. 1990. Spirituality: An untapped resource for hope and coping in family caregivers of individuals with cancer. Oncology Nursing Forum (abstract) 17(2):159
Objective: Explores the dimension of spirituality and its relationship with depression among family caregivers. *Sample & Methods*: Convenience sample of 100 family caregivers of patients age 18 or older with a solid tumor and under cancer treatment. Data were collected on caregivers every 3 months for a period of 1 year. The Spiritual/Philosophical Subscale from the Coping Resources Inventory was used to assess spirituality; the CES-D measured depressive symptoms. *Results*: Spirituality was inversely related to depression (r = -.24, p < .001). *Conclusions*: Caregivers may utilize spirituality as a coping resource when they deal with the difficult experience of caring for a family member with cancer. *Quality*: Good.

124. Pressman, P., J.S. Lyons, D.B. Larson, J.J. Strain. 1990. Religious belief, depression, and ambulation status in elderly women with broken hips. American Journal of Psychiatry 147:758-760.
Objective: Explores the relationship between religious belief, depression status, and physical disability status in hospitalized elderly patients.

Sample & Methods: The sample consisted of 30 women age 65 years or older (without a psychiatric history or cognitive impairment) who were recovering from surgical repair of a broken hip on the orthopedic service of a large midwestern teaching hospital (Northwestern University, Chicago, Illinois). Religious belief was measured using the Index of Religiousness (IOR) (frequency of church attendance, perceived religiousness, and religion is a source of strength and comfort); depression by the Geriatric Depression Scale (GDS); ambulation status by a physical therapist who measured "meters walked at discharge. GDS was administered at two points in time: within 48 hrs of surgery and just prior to discharge; all the remaining scales (including IOR) were administered just prior to discharge. *Results*: Religiosity (IOR) was inversely related to discharge depression score ($r = -0.61$, $p < .01$); this relationship persisted even after controlling for severity of illness. Religiosity was also positively correlated with meters walked at discharge ($r = +0.45$, $p < .05$). The third item of the IOR, strength and comfort derived from religion (religious coping), was inversely related to both post-surgery depression score and discharge depression score. *Conclusions*: Religious belief was associated with lower levels of depression and better ambulation status in elderly women recovering from hip fracture. *Quality*: Good; small sample, but strikingly large correlations.

125. Johnson, S.C., and B. Spilka. 1991. Coping with breast cancer: the roles of clergy and faith. Journal of Religion and Health 30(1):21-33.

Objective: Examines the relationship between personal religious orientation and coping with breast cancer, and the role that clergy play in providing support to women with this condition. *Sample & Methods*: 103 cancer patients (mean age 53) were recruited from American Cancer Society support groups. Religiousness was measured using Allport's Intrinsic-Extrinsic Religiosity Scale. Items measuring self-perception of emotion and coping with cancer were asked; a validated measure of emotional state or coping was not used. *Results*: 85% of the women reported that religion helped them to cope. Intrinsic religiousness was strongly correlated with successful coping ($r = .70$, $p < .01$), but extrinsic religiosity was unrelated. *Conclusions*: The clergy can play an important role in helping women with breast cancer to cope more effectively with their illness. High levels of intrinsic religiosity facilitate adaptation. *Quality*: Good.

126. Saudia, T.L., M.R. Kinnery, K.C. Brown, and L. Young-Ward. 1991. Health locus of control and helpfulness of prayer. Heart and Lung 20:60-65.

Objective: To determine whether "locus of control" affects whether or not coronary artery bypass surgery (CABS) patients find prayer helpful. *Sample & Methods*: 100 patients awaiting CABS (75% male, 87% Protestant) at the University of Alabama in Birmingham, were surveyed using the Multidimensional Health Locus of Control scale and the Helpfulness of Prayer Scale (HPS). Locus of control was categorized as "internal", "chance", or "powerful other"; helpfulness of prayer was rated on a 0-15 scale. *Results*: 96% of patients indicated they used prayer as a coping mechanism; 97% rated prayer to be very helpful and 70% gave it the top score of 15 on the HPS. Helpfulness of prayer was not related to locus of control. *Conclusions*: Irrespective of a person's locus of control, prayer is an important coping behavior used to deal with potentially life-threatening medical problems. *Quality*: Very good. Many of the patients in this study were older adults.

127. Harris R.C., M.A. Dew, A. Lee, M. Amaya, L. Buches, D. Reetz, and G. Coleman. 1992. The role of religion in heart transplant recipients' health and well-being. Paper presented at the 3rd biannual Conference on Psychiatric, Psychosocial, and Ethical Issues in Organ Transplantation, Pittsburgh, Penn, May 1992.

Objective: Systematically examines the role of religion in the adjustment of patients to heart transplantation. *Sample and Methods*: 40 adult cardiac transplant recipients were followed during the first 12 months post-surgery; three-quarters were over age 45, 80% were male, 56% had at least some college or vocational school, and 50% had an income greater than $30,000/yr. A wide range of religious beliefs and practices were measured. Well-being, self-esteem, health worries, anger, and difficulty with the medical regimen (compliance) were measured using acceptable scales. *Results*: Religiosity tended to decrease over time, with the highest levels measured at 2 months post-transplant and the lowest levels at the 12-month interview. At the 2nd month interview, self-esteem was positively related to frequency of private prayer and activity level within the church; "health worries" were inversely related to religious beliefs and church attendance. At the 7th month interview, self-esteem was again positively related to religiosity, especially "influence of beliefs" and "financial contributions to church". At the 12 month interview, self-esteem was again positively related to activity level within the church; health worries were inversely related to activity within the congregation and frequency of church attendance; level of anger was inversely related to influence of religious beliefs on life; and difficulties with compliance were inversely related to influence of beliefs and private prayer. *Conclusions*: Heart transplant recipients with stronger beliefs and more frequent religious activities experienced better physical and emotional well-being, fewer health worries, and better medical compliance by the final 12 month assessment. *Quality*: Very good. Important data from a rarely studied group of medical patients.

128. Idler, E.L., and S.V. Kasl. 1992. Religion, disability, depression, and the timing of death. <u>American Journal of Sociology</u> 97:1052-1079.

Objective: Examines the prospective relationship between religious involvement and health status (depression, disability, and mortality). *Sample & Methods*: Stratified probability sample (n = 2,812) of adults aged 65 or over, dwelling independently in the community of New Haven, Connecticut (same baseline sample as 1987 report). Initially surveyed in 1982, this cohort was followed up in 1983, 1984, and 1985; mortality data was available through 1989 for this report; note that nearly 37% of subjects (1,037) interviewed in 1982 had died by January 1989 (indicating the degree of medical illness in this population). *Results*: Subjects who were highly involved with their church or synagogue in 1982 were significantly less likely to be disabled one, two, and three years later; this effect persisted after controlling for health behaviors, social networks, and general attitudes. This effect was true primarily for Catholics, less so for Jews, and not at all true for Protestants. The effect was due both to improvement of functional disability and to prevention of decline. Public or private religiousness in 1982, however, had no impact on 1985 depression scores; rather, the most important variables predicting depression were disability in 1982 and change in disability between 1982 and 1985. Sex-specific effects were notable. Religious coping (strength and comfort from religion) protected men with worsening disability from becoming depressed in 1985, even after controlling for 1982 disability. Data on mortality demonstrated no ability for either private or public religiousness in 1982 to predict survival. Among both Christians and Jews, however, there were significantly lower death rates 30 days before their respective major holidays than during the 30 days afterward. *Conclusion*: Religion plays a profound, but complicated role in the physical and emotional lives of older adults. For men, religion has a buffering effect, reducing the probability that they will become depressed following disability. *Quality*: Excellent.

(54.) Koenig, H.G., H.J. Cohen, D.G. Blazer, C. Pieper, K.G. Meador. F. Shelp, V. Goli, and R. DiPasquale. 1992. Religious coping and depression among elderly, hospitalized medically ill men. <u>American Journal of Psychiatry</u> 149:1693-1700.
      [Reviewed in Part I.]

Objective: Examines the cross-sectional and longitudinal relationship between religious coping (dependence on religion to help relieve stress) and depression in older adults acutely hospitalized with medical illness. *Sample & Methods*: 850 consecutively hospitalized men age 65 or over were assessed within 48 to 72 hrs of admission using the 3-item Religious Coping Index (RCI), the self-rated Geriatric Depression Scale (GDS), and the clinician-rated Hamilton Depression Scale. A subgroup of patients were then followed an average of 6 months after discharge to assess both religious coping and depression. *Results*: After controlling for 15 other sociodemographic and health factors, religious coping (prayer, reading the Bible, faith or trust in God) was inversely related to both self-rated (p<.0001) and clinician-rated (p=.0005) depression scores at baseline. When 202 patients were followed up 6 months after discharge, only three variables predicted depression outcome (once other variables were controlled): (1) baseline depression score (+0.62), (2) a medical diagnosis of kidney disease (+0.15), and (3) baseline religious coping (RCI score) (-0.18, p $\leq$ .01). Finally, change in religious coping and change in depression score were unrelated (r=+.06, p>.40). *Conclusion*: Religious coping was inversely related to depression cross-sectionally, predicted lower depression scores on longitudinal followup, and there was no association between change in religious coping and change in depression score. The inverse relationship between religious coping and depression reflects religion's capacity to protect against or facilitate resolution of depression in this setting, and cannot be explained by a lessening of religious faith caused by increased depression. Provides evidence to support a causal link between Judeo-Christian religious coping and positive adaptation.

129.   Koenig, H.G., H.J. Cohen, D.G. Blazer, and K.R.R. Krishnan. 1995. Religious coping and cognitive symptoms of depression in elderly medical patients. Psychosomatics, in press.

Objective: Examines the association between religious coping and depressive symptom "type" in medically ill older adults. *Sample & Methods*: 850 consecutively admitted men age 65 or over to the medical and neurological services (77% response rate); mean age 70 years, 28% Black, mean education 9 yrs, 68% married. Religious coping was evaluated using the Religious Coping Index. Depressive symptoms were measured using the Schedule for Affective Disorders and Schizophrenia (symptom severity), the Hamilton Depression Scale, and the Geriatric Depression Scale. *Results*: Cognitive symptoms of depression, but not somatic symptoms, were related to religious coping; boredom, loss of interest, social withdrawal, feeling downhearted and blue, restlessness, feeling like a failure, feeling helpless or hopeless or feeling that other people were better off, were all less common among men who depended heavily on religion to cope. *Conclusions*: Religious coping is associated with fewer cognitive, but not somatic, symptoms of depression. For mild or moderate depression (often associated with cognitive symptoms), religious strategies may be helpful for preventing or relieving symptoms; when depression severity reaches a the point where somatic symptoms emerge, religious strategies may be less helpful.

Chronic Mentally Ill

130. Chu, C. and H.E. Klein. 1985. Psychosocial and environmental variables in outcome of Black schizophrenics. Journal of the National Medical Association 77:793-796.
Objective: Examines psychosocial and environmental variables associated with rehospitalization of Black schizophrenics after discharge. *Sample & Methods*: Of 275 schizophrenic patients consecutively admitted to seven hospitals and mental health centers of the Missouri Division of Mental Health, 47% (128) were Black patients who comprised the sample for this study; subject characteristics included 51% urban residence, 54% men, and mean age 34 years (range 17 to 57 years). *Results*: Urban Black schizophrenics were less likely to be rehospitalized if they said prayers once daily rather than more often (chisquare 8.0, $p < .05$). On the other hand, they were also less likely to be readmitted if their families encouraged them to continue religious worship while in the hospital (chisquare 12.0, $p < .001$). For all Black patients, they were more likely to be rehospitalized if family had no religious affiliation (chisquare 8.7, $p < .025$). *Conclusions*: The findings suggest a positive association between religious worship and favorable outcomes for Black schizophrenic patients. *Quality*: Good. While this study does not include elderly schizophrenics, it provides information that may be applicable to that group (about which almost nothing is known).

131. Kroll, J., and W. Sheehan. 1989. Religious beliefs and practices among 52 psychiatric inpatients in Minnesota. American Journal of Psychiatry 146:67-72.
Objective: Examines the religious characteristics of psychiatric inpatients, mostly with chronic mental illness. *Sample & Methods*: The sample was composed of 52 patients (two-thirds women, one-third over the age of 35, two-thirds with a high school education or more). Psychiatric diagnoses included major depression (31%), bipolar disorder (21%), schizophrenia (19%), and personality disorder (19%). Detailed information on religious beliefs, practices and experiences were

collected. *Results*: Belief in God, the Devil, and an afterlife were uniformly high. Patients with depression or anxiety disorders scored lower on a wide range of religious measures than did those with other psychiatric diagnoses. *Conclusions*: Religion is an important factor in the lives of most of these psychiatric inpatients, and deserves further study. *Quality*: Good. While not specifically addressing issues in elderly adults, their sample includes older persons and the results may be generalizable to this age group.

132. Guarnaccia, P.J., P. Parra, A. Deschamps, G. Milstein, and N. Argiles. 1992. Si dios quiere: Hispanic families' experiences of caring for a seriously mentally ill family member. <u>Culture, Medicine and Psychiatry</u> 16(2):187-215.

Objective: Examines minority families' conceptions of serious mental illnesses, their interactions with the mental health system, and the burdens experienced while caring for chronically mentally ill relatives. *Sample & Methods*: Case reports (New Jersey). *Results & Conclusions*: Religion plays an important role in providing support to caregivers; both religious institutions and religious healings were found to be a major source of solace. *Quality*: Good. While not specifically dealing with an elderly population, this is one of the few studies to address religion as a support for caregivers of chronically mentally ill patients.

Death Anxiety

133. Richardson, V., S. Berman, and M. Piwowarski. 1983. Projective assessment of the relationships between the salience of death, religion, and age among adults in America. <u>Journal of General Psychology</u> 109:149-156.

Objective: Investigates relationships between age, religious orientation, and perceptions of death. *Sample & Methods*: Random national sample of 1428 adults age 21 yrs or older in United States. Trained interviewers from University of Michigan Survey Research Center conducted a 90 minute interview during which they were administered a thematic apperceptive procedure modeled after the Thematic Apperception Test. A total of 12 thematic apperceptive pictures were shown and respondents asked to tell a story. The total number of "death-related" stories were calculated for each respondent. Respondents were dichotomized into those with and without a religious preference. Sample was divided into three age groups (21-34, 35-54, and 55+). *Results*: A statistically significant association (p<.02) was found between references to death and no religious preference (13%

of those with no religious preference and 5% of those with a preference). An interaction with age was present such that this relationship was true only among younger participants, but not in the elderly. *Conclusions*: The link between religiosity and concerns about death decrease with age; this has implications for the relationship between death anxiety and religion. *Quality*: Fair.

134. Koenig, H.G. 1988. Religious behaviors and death anxiety in later life. Hospice Journal 4(1):3-24.
Objective: Explores the relationship between death anxiety and use of religious beliefs and prayer to cope during stress. *Sample & Methods*: Questionnaire sent by mail to 263 senior center participants and 41 home-bound elderly living in mid-Missouri (43% response rate). A single item measured death anxiety. Two items measured use of religious beliefs and prayer during stress. *Results*: Respondents very likely to use religious beliefs and prayer during stress were significantly less likely to report fear and anxiety about death (10% vs 24% of others, p<.01). Relationships were strongest for women and those age 75 or older. *Conclusions*: Religious beliefs and prayer are particularly important for women and those age 75 or older in dealing with the fear and anxiety surrounding death.

135. Thorson, J.A., and F.C. Powell. 1989. Death anxiety and religion in an older male sample. Psychological Reports 64(3 Pt 1):985-986.
Objective: These renowned mental health experts examine the relationship between death anxiety and intrinsic religiosity in an older sample. *Sample & Methods*: The sample was composed of 103 elderly men. A multi-dimensional death anxiety scale (based on the work of Templer) was used to measure death anxiety; Hoge's Intrinsic Religiosity Scale was used to measure religiosity. *Results & Conclusions*: While death anxiety was inversely related to intrinsic religiosity (r=-.11), the association did not achieve statistical significance. *Quality*: Good. The authors themselves note in a later paper that this nonsignificant result may have been due to "data compaction in a homogeneous sample." In a more recent study using a heterogenous sample of persons aged 18 to 88 years, they found death anxiety low and intrinsic religiosity high among older adults; in that report, there was a significant inverse relationship between intrinsic religiosity and death anxiety [Thorson, J.A., Powell, F.C. (1990). Meanings of death and intrinsic religiosity. Journal of Clinical Psychology 46, 379-391].

136. Thorson, J.A., and F.C. Powell. 1991. Life, death, and life after
        death: Meanings of the relationship between death anxiety and
        religion. Journal of Religious Gerontology 8(1):41-56.
Objective: Examines and seeks to explain the relationship between
death anxiety, religious beliefs, and religious practices. *Sample &
Methods*: A purposive sample recruited from Omaha, Nebraska,
included 65 high school students, 48 undergraduates, 29 graduate
students, 128 continuing education students, and 119 persons
attending a university senior citizens' day (N = 389); 81% were women
and 91% were White. *Results*: Women who either attended church
infrequently or did not describe themselves as religious had significantly
higher death anxiety. Participants troubled by the uncertainty of an
afterlife experienced the highest death anxiety; older persons had the
highest belief in an after life and as a group had the lowest death
anxiety. Depth of religious belief was more important than religious
activities in predicting lower death anxiety. *Conclusions*: Death
anxiety was highest among young women with low religious beliefs
and activities; death anxiety was lowest among older adults, the most
religious component of the sample. *Quality*: Good. Emphasizes the
importance of religious beliefs and attitudes (especially for women) in
allaying death anxiety.

See also:

89. Koenig et al. 1993. Journal of Geriatric Psychiatry 26 (1):65-93.

Alcoholism

137.   Larson, D.B., and W.P. Wilson. 1980.   Religious life of
         alcoholics. Southern Medical Journal 73:723-727.
Objective: Investigates the present and early religious life of alcoholics.
Sample & Methods: The sample was composed of 81 men (cases)
admitted to the psychiatric units at John Umstead State Hospital in
Butner, North Carolina, and the VA Medical Center in Durham, North
Carolina; 107 normal controls were recruited from the same geographic
area as the cases. Forty-one percent of cases and 42% of controls
were over the age of 50. Social class differences were prominent
between the two groups. *Results*: The majority of alcoholics came
from broken homes (70% vs 20% for controls, $p < .01$). Controls were
more likely to have been raised in an environment with a conservative
religious belief system. The mothers of the alcoholics attended church
more regularly than did mothers of the controls; on the other hand, the
fathers of the controls attended more regularly than the fathers of the

alcoholics. During their teen years, 89% of alcoholics lost interest in religion; in contrast, this occurred in only 20% of normal controls, where interest in religion increased in 48% and remained the same in another 32% (p<.01). Seventy-five percent of controls reported having a salvation experience at some point in their lives, whereas only 46% of alcoholics reported this. Finally, only 3% of alcoholics had ever shared their faith publicly with others, whereas 50% of normal controls had done this. *Conclusions*: Alcoholics came from homes where parents did not have the same religious practices, where religious beliefs were not well integrated into daily living, where religion was not translated into practical benefits, and where there was conflict between what parents taught children about religion and what the church taught them. *Quality*: Good. Wonder if these results would have come out the same if the analyses had been control for the rather marked differences in social class between cases and controls.

138. Alexander, F., and R.W. Duff. 1991. Influence of religiosity and alcohol use on personal well-being. Journal of Religious Gerontology 8(2):11-21.

Objective: Examines the relationships between life satisfaction, religiosity, social interaction, and alcohol use among members of a secular and a religious retirement community. *Sample & Methods*: Participants came from two adjoining Southern California communities: one composed of upper-middle class retired professionals (academics, physicians, economists, etc.) (n=450) and the other composed of retired ministers, missionaries, and religious educators (n=320). The modal religious denomination for both communities was Congregational. A random sample of 256 persons was selected from residential lists; 62 were excluded because of illness and 35 refused to participate, leaving a final sample of 156 subjects. Characteristics of the 75 participants from the secular community were: mean age 82, 33% male, 47% married, median income $39,136/yr; characteristic for the 81 subjects from the religious community: mean age 77, 37% male, 66% married, median income $24,562/yr. *Results*: When compared with the secular community, members of the religious community had significantly higher levels of life satisfaction and social interaction (t=2.4, p<.01, and t=2.3, p<.01), whereas alcohol use and death anxiety were significantly lower (t=3.1, p<.01, and t=4.2, p<.01). *Conclusions*: Religiosity may play a direct impact on feelings of personal well-being after retirement. *Quality*: Very good. Unique study comparing secular and religious retirement communities, though statistical methods relatively simplistic. Also one of the few studies of this nature performed on the West coast.

139. Krause, N. 1991. Stress, religiosity, and abstinence from
      alcohol. Psychology and Aging 6:134-144.
Objective: Renowned public health researcher from University of
Michigan tests a conceptual model that examines psychosocial
variables related to abstinence from alcohol in later life; both life
stressors and coping resources were examined. *Sample & Methods*:
Data are from the Americans' Changing Lives Survey (Michigan Survey
Research Center, 1986), which used a multistage stratified method to
identify a random national sample of 3,617 adults (including an
oversample of Blacks and elderly); 1,669 participants were aged 60 or
over, who comprised the sample for this report. LISREL VII was used
to examine relationships between variables. *Results*: Greater physical
health problems, lower education, and male sex were associated with
a greater likelihood of abstinence from alcohol. Unrelated were age,
race or financial difficulty. Subjective religiosity, but not frequency of
church attendance, was significantly related to abstinence in this
model. *Conclusions*: Greater subjective religiosity is associated with a
greater probability that elderly people will abstain from using alcohol.
Quality: Excellent.

140. Koenig, H.G., L.K. George, K.G. Meador, D.G. Blazer, and S.M.
      Ford. 1994. Religious practices and alcoholism in a southern
      adult population. Hospital & Community Psychiatry 45:225-
      231.
Objective: Examines the relationship between religion (affiliation and
practices) and alcohol abuse-dependence in young, middle-aged, and
elderly persons. *Sample & Methods*: Data on 2,969 adults from the
1983-84 NIMH Epidemiologic Catchment Area survey (Piedmont site,
North Carolina) were examined for associations between religion and
alcoholism. Religious variables included church attendance, Bible-
reading and prayer, importance of religion, "born again" status, and
religious affiliation. Alcohol abuse-dependence was diagnosed using
the Diagnostic Interview Schedule which uses DSM-III criteria; 6-month
and lifetime rates of alcoholism were examined. *Results*: Frequent
church attenders had lower recent (6-month) and lifetime rates of
alcoholism. Recent alcoholism was also less frequent among those
who read the Bible and prayed frequently. On the other hand, alcoholic
disorders were more common among those who frequently watch
religious TV or listened to religious radio. Finally, lifetime alcohol
disorders (but not recent) were more common among those with
Pentecostal affiliations. These relationships were strongest in adults
aged 18 to 39, and weakened among middle-aged and elderly adults.
Conclusions: Alcohol abuse and dependence are inversely associated
with communal and private religious behaviors, particularly in younger

adults. Religion may buffer against the onset of alcoholism or may help persons to achieve abstinence once an addictive pattern has begun. The positive association between alcoholism and religious TV/radio requires further study.

Suicide

141. Stack, S. 1983. The effect of religious commitment on suicide: A cross-sectional analysis. Journal of Health and Social Behavior 24:362-374.
Objective: Examined suicide rates in countries around the world, comparing them to the religiousness of those countries. *Sample & Methods*: 25 countries were examined. Religiousness was determined by religious book production rates in each country. *Results*: Suicide rates were inversely proportional to religiosity. These findings were particularly strong among women over age 65 and men aged 65 to 74. *Conclusions*: There is an inverse relationship between religiousness and suicide rates in this gross cross-sectional examination, particularly among older adults. *Quality*: Good.

142. Martin, W.T. 1984. Religiosity and United States suicide rates, 1972-1978. Journal of Clinical Psychology 40:1166-1169.
Objective: Examines the association between annual variations in suicide rates between 1972 and 1978 as a function of church attendance. *Sample & Methods*: Suicide rates per 100,000 between 1972-1978 were obtained from DHHS; religious involvement was based on General Social Surveys conducted by NORC. The mean church attendance for white males, black males, white females, black females was correlated with the corresponding suicide rates for each subpopulation. *Results*: A significant negative correlation between suicide rates and church attendance was found ($r = -.85$, $p < .0001$). Despite differences in religious involvement among the different subpopulations, church attendance was equally effective as a deterrent to suicide for all groups. *Conclusions*: These data support the notion that religion deters suicide. A sociological explanation is that religious involvement accomplishes this through group cohesiveness; a psychological explanation is that religious involvement is effective because it enhances psychic cohesiveness (integration of conscious with unconscious mind). *Quality*: Good. Although all ages are considered, these results likely apply to the elderly as well.

143. Lester, D. 1988. Religion and personal violence (homicide and suicide) in the USA. Psychological Reports 62:618.

Objective: Examines relationships between suicide and homicide rates, religious affiliation, and church attendance. *Sample & Methods*: Percentage of Catholics and church attenders in each state were correlated with suicide and homicide rates. *Results*: Suicide rates were inversely correlated with both church attendance (partial $r = -.54$, $p < .001$) and with Roman Catholicism (partial $r = -.23$). Homicide rates were inversely correlated with church attendance (partial $r = -.30$, $p < .05$) but not Catholicism. *Conclusions*: Church attendance is a much stronger predictor of suicide and homicide than is denomination. *Quality*: Good. Again, while not specifically dealing with elders, results likely to apply to this age group with the highest of all suicide rates.

144. Koenig, H.G. 1994. Self-destructive behaviors related to death in physically ill elderly men: Pilot data. Unpublished paper. Duke University Medical Center, Durham, North Carolina 27710.

Objective: Examines the relationship between religious coping and suicidal thoughts among physically ill older men. *Sample & Methods*: 332 men age 70 or over consecutively admitted to a VA medical center. Suicidal thoughts measured with one item on the Montgomery-Asberg Depression Scale. Religious coping measured using a 3-item (Religious Coping Index). *Results*: 18% had rare or more frequent suicidal thoughts. Suicidal thoughts were inversely related to religious coping. *Conclusions*: Religious cognitions may help to allay thoughts of suicide in physically ill older men (the group with the highest known suicide rate in the U.S.). Note that a cross-sectional study like this probably underestimates religion's effects on preventing suicide, since many non-religious older men with depression may have already committed suicide and not be available for sampling, whereas depressed religious elders may have survived but still have suicidal thoughts that their beliefs have prevented them from acting on.

Adjusting to Prison

145. Panton, J.H. 1979. An MMPI item content scale to measure religious identification within a state prison population. Journal of Clinical Psychology 35:588-591.

Objective: Examines the relationship between religion and adjustment to prison life in a sample of state prison inmates. *Sample & Methods*: Sample consisted of 117 adjusted and 117 non-adjusted inmates at Central Prison in Raleigh, North Carolina. Age of participants was not reported. Religiousness was based on an item content scale (RI scale) developed from the MMPI that reflected identification with and participation in religious activities. *Results*: A significant difference was found between adjusted and non-adjusted prisoners (Student $t = 21.34$, $p < .001$), with adjusted prisoners scoring higher on religiosity. These results were replicated in a separate sample of 100 adjusted and 100 maladjusted prisoners ($t = 20.45$, $p < .001$). *Conclusions*: Religion plays an important role in the adjustment of inmates to prison life. *Quality*: Good.

See also:

11. Koenig, H.G. 1995. Religion and older men in prison. International Journal of Geriatric Psychiatry, in press.

Marital and Sexual Issues

146. Robinson, L.C. 1994. Religious orientation in enduring marriage: An exploratory study. Review of Religious Research 35:207-218.

Objective: Examines what older couples say are the key ingredients to long and successful marriages. *Sample & Methods*: Fifteen couples (30 subjects) were asked to discuss the strengths of their marital relationships (Oklahoma State University). Two-thirds of the couples were Protestant. Mean age of husbands was 64 years (range 55-70 years) and of wives was 62 years (range 54-67). Couples had been married an average of 40 years. The majority had attended college and one-third currently had an income of $35,000/yr or more. *Results*: Presented in qualitative terms. Most subjects indicated their religious faith was an important strength that enhanced their marital relationship; religion enhanced other strengths such as intimacy, commitment, and communication. *Quality*: Good. References are excellent. One of the few studies on this important topic in the elderly.

147. Koenig, H.G., and S. Herman. 1995. Religion and coping with sexual impotence in later life. Journal of Religious Gerontology, in press.

Objective: Examines the relationship between adjustment to sexual impotence and religious characteristics of older men. *Sample & Methods*: This was a consecutive sample of 83 men aged 55 or older with sexual dysfunction seen for psychological evaluation in a urology clinic at Duke University Medical Center. Religious denomination and church attendance were correlated with sexual practices, help-seeking behaviors, and psychological adjustment. *Results*: Older men who were affiliated with conservative Protestant denominations and those who were frequent church attenders were more likely to be involved in a variety of help-seeking behaviors, and were more likely to perceive their partners as supporting their attempts to seek help. There was not evidence, however that conservative religious affiliation or frequent church attendance protected against psychological distress. Of particular concern was that this group used a more restricted range of sexual behaviors to facilitate arousal and improve partner satisfaction. *Conclusions*: Counselors seeing older men with psychological distress and sexual dysfunction should encourage them to engage in a wider range of behaviors to facilitate partner satisfaction.

Caregiving in Alzheimer's Disease

148.   Hall, G.R. (Task Force Chairperson) and B.L. Grandquist (Executive Director, Iowa Department of Elder Affairs). Iowa Governor's Task Force on Alzheimer's Disease and Related Disorders Final Report, November 1989, p 115.

Objective: Survey of Alzheimer's caregivers on their attitudes, including the role of religion. *Sample & Methods*: Large community sample, exact size unknown. *Results*: When asked why they had chosen a caregiver role, 92% of caregivers indicated that "giving care is the Christian thing to do and not to do so is morally wrong"; 92% indicated that God helps in their efforts as caregivers and 44% expected to be rewarded for their caregiving. *Conclusions*: Religious cognitions play an important role in chosing and continuing in the caregiver role. *Quality*: Good. Those wishing to know further about this work may wish to contact Jacqueline M. Stolley, Certified Gerontological Nurse, 2942 Iowa St, Davenport, Iowa 52803.

149. Rabins, P.V., M.D. Fitting, J. Esatham, and J. Zabora. 1990. Emotional adaptation over time in caregivers for chronically ill elderly people. Age and Aging 19:185-190.

Objective: Examines factors which predict emotional adaptation in caregivers of elders with Alzheimer's disease or recurrent metastatic cancer. *Sample & Methods*: 32 caregivers of patients with Alzheimer's disease and 30 caregivers of patients with metastatic cancer were interviewed three times over a two-year period. Emotional adaptation was measured in terms of decline in negative affect score and increase in positive affect score during the study period. Multiple regression was used to control for confounding variables. *Results*: Self-reported low strength of religious beliefs, caregiver neuroticism, and anger explained 54% of the variance of negative affect scores; high number of social contacts and strong self-reported religious faith explained

43% of the variance of positive affect scores. *Conclusions*: Self-reported strength of religious belief is an important predictor of emotional adaptation in caregivers of chronically ill older adults. *Quality*: Very Good.

150. Wood, J.B. and I.A. Parham. 1990. Coping with perceived burden: Ethnic and cultural issues in Alzheimer's family caregiving. Journal of Applied Gerontology 9:325-239.

Objective: Investigates different patterns of coping with caregiver strain seen among Black and White, rural and urban families. *Sample & Methods*: Convenience sample (selected on the basis of race and residence) of 85 women who were primary caregivers to relatives diagnosed with Alzheimer's disease; mean age 60 years; 37% spouse caregivers, 26% child caregivers; 42% Black and 61% urban. Relative Stress Scale was used to assess personal distress, life upset, and negative feelings toward elders. Action-oriented (behavioral) and cognitive coping strategies were assessed using measures developed by Conway (1985) and were expanded to include additional religious items. *Results*: Blacks were particularly likely to consider God a part of their support system; God was perceived in a very personal way, just as family, friends, and neighbors were. God was involved in every aspect of care, including the physical care. Thus, a personal concept of God was important for Blacks, particularly urban Blacks, as a cognitive coping strategy. *Conclusions*: Black caregivers use a broad range of informal supports, including the important support of a deity perceived in a very personal way. *Quality*: Good.

151. Whitlatch, A.M., D.I. Meddaugh, and K.J. Langhout. 1992. Religiosity among Alzheimer's disease caregivers. American Journal of Alzheimer's Disease and Related Disorders & Research, November/December issue: 11-20.

Objective: Examines the role of religiosity in enabling Alzheimer's disease caregivers to cope with their caregiving tasks. *Sample & Methods*: Sample was composed of 31 Alzheimer's Association family members from a midwestern U.S. community (Ohio). They were interviewed during a support group meeting. Qualitative statements made by caregivers were categorized into knowledge of AD, caregiving problems and strategies, resources, and feelings. *Results*: Religiosity was found to be a pervading theme across all categories that were examined. Statements were discussed in terms of organizational, non-organizational, and intrinsic forms of religiosity. *Conclusions*: The importance of religion in enabling these caregivers to cope indicates a need for further research to determine the extent and nature of religion's use in this setting. *Quality*: Good. A small study, but provides important qualitative data that should help to formulate questions to be examined in future research.

General Mental Health

152. Levin, J.S. 1988. Religious factors in aging, adjustment, and health: A theoretical overview. Journal of Religion and Aging 4 (3-4):133-146.
Objective: Reviews empirical findings from recent research on the relationship between religiosity and health in later life to determine which theoretical orientation is most accurate for aging adults: disengagement theory, activity theory, the social isolation model, an eschatological view, and so forth. *Sample & Methods*: Literature review and theoretical discussion. *Results & Conclusions*: The multidimensional disengagement perspective of Mindel and Vaughan appears to best fit the findings from research. Church attendance remains stable over a person's life course, declining slightly in the very old or the disabled. Likewise, non-organizational religious activities like prayer or scripture reading remain stable with age, with only a slight increase in later life to compensate for declining church attendance. The positive association between church attendance and both physical and psychological well-being also remains the same throughout the life cycle. Church attendance, however, may represent a proxy for health status among the very old. *Quality*: Very good.

153. Johnson, D.P., and L.C. Mullins. 1989. Religiosity and loneliness among the elderly. Journal of Applied Gerontology 8:110-131.
Objective: Analyzes the relationship between loneliness and two dimensions of religiosity (social and subjective). *Sample & Methods*: Interviews were conducted with 131 residents of a highrise senior housing facility; sampling method not specified, but all subjects were 62 years or older (mean age, 76), 76% were female, 88% were white, and 54% had less than a high school education. Regression models are used to control for relevant covariates. *Results*: The social dimension (membership, attendance, church member visits) was inversely related to loneliness, where as the subjective dimension (religious importance and prayer) was unrelated to loneliness (although in the hypothesized direction). *Conclusions*: Older persons who are more involved in the social aspects of their church are less likely to be lonely. *Quality*: Fair.

154. Maton, K.I. 1989. The stress-buffering role of spiritual support: Cross-sectional and prospective investigations. Journal for the

Scientific Study of Religion 28:310-323.
Objective: Examines the contribution of spiritual support to well-being under conditions of high versus low stress. *Sample & Methods*: Presents the results from two studies: #1 "Life stress in bereaved parents" and #2 "Life stress in the first semester of college." In study #1, the sample was composed of 81 members of support groups for bereaved parents (average age 46 years, 77% female, mostly White). Spiritual support was measured with a 3-item scale: "I experience God's love and caring on a regular basis," "I experience a close personal relationship with God," and "Religious faith has not been central to my coping." High life stress was defined as one whose child had died within past two years (n=33) and low stress if death occurred more than two years (n=48). Social support, depression (Hopkins Symptom Checklist), and the usual demographics were measured. In study #2, 68 recently graduated high school seniors at University of Maryland were recruited and surveyed prior to entering college and 10 weeks after entering college. Same spiritual support measure was used as in 1st study. High stress was defined as 3 or more stressful life events in past 6 months; low stress was defined as 2 or fewer of such events. Depression and social support were also measured. *Results*: Study #1 (bereaved parents). For the high stress subsample, spiritual support was inversely related to Depression (r = -.33, p<.05) and positively related to high Self-Esteem (r = +.42, p<.01). In the low stress subsample, spiritual support was unrelated to either variable. These results and further analyses revealed substantive evidence for a distinct, buffering effect for spiritual support in the high-stress subsample. Study #2 (college students). For the high stress subsample, spiritual support was positively and significantly related to personal-emotional adjustment (r=.47, p<.01), whereas in the low stress subsample, there was no correlation (r=.00). *Conclusions*: Individuals who are under high levels of personal stress are especially likely to benefit from spiritual support. *Quality*: Very good. This is a most important study that has relevance to the elderly. Community studies of older adults that examine the relationship between religion and well-being must take into account the differential effects that religion may have depending on whether subjects are under high or low stress. For this reason, the relationship between religion and well-being may be best demonstrated in clinical samples (physically ill older adults).

155. Wong, P.T.P. 1989. Personal meaning and successful aging.
     Canadian Psychology 30:516-525.
Objective: Examines the concept of "personal meaning," its relationship connection with spirituality, and its role in successful aging. *Sample*

& *Methods*: Literature review and discussion. *Results & Conclusions*: Personal meaning is an existential need. Sources of meaning (work, social status, activity) are often threatened in later life. Yet health and life satisfaction are closely tied to the person's ability to maintain personal meaning, despite these losses. When the usual sources of meaning are lost, the older adult may discover meaning by tapping inner and spiritual resources. Four stages are described in response to illness, pain, and personal death: reminiscence, commitment, personal optimism, and religiosity and spiritual well-being. *Quality*: Very good.

156. Koenig, H.G. 1990. Research on religion and mental health in later life: A review and commentary. Journal of Geriatric Psychiatry 23:23-53.
Objective: Provides a overview of the topic of religion and mental health in the elderly, summarizing and commenting on relevant studies. *Sample & Methods*: Literature review and discussion. *Results & Conclusions*: There has been a long, antagonistic relationship between psychology and religion. Despite this negative relationship, religious beliefs and behaviors are highly prevalent in later life. There are many studies that demonstrate an association between religious factors and mental health in this population; religion also appears to have a positive impact on functional disability and the experience of pain. Finally, the influence of religion on the doctor-patient relationship is explored, and implications for clinicians are discussed.

157. Smith, C.H. 1991. Adrienne Rich, Ruth Whitman, and their Jewish elders. International Journal of Aging and Human Development 33:203-209.
Objective: Discusses two American poets' depiction of their Jewish elders and the effects that maintaining or suppressing ties to Judaism can have on adaptation in late life. *Sample & Methods*: Reviews poems by Rich and Whitman that refer to their Jewish grandparents and the effects of either maintaining or severing ties to their Jewish heritage. *Results & Conclusions*: There is evidence that some elders who suppress their ties to Judaism suffer psychologically as they age; however, even those who maintain these ties can experience depression. Likewise, some Jews who completely reject their Jewish heritage in later life adapt relatively well. Heterogeneity of psychological responses to maintaining or severing ties to Judaism was the rule. *Quality*: Fair.

158. Walton, C.G., C.M. Shultz, C.M. Beck, and R.C. Walls. 1991. Psychological correlates of loneliness in the older adult. Archives of Psychiatric Nursing 5(3):165-170.

Objective: Assesses the relationship between loneliness, hopelessness, and spiritual well-being. *Sample & Methods*: This was a convenience sample of 107 persons aged 61-91. Loneliness was predicted using a "regression decision tree with automatic random subset cross-validation." *Results & Conclusions*: Loneliness was positively associated with loss and hopelessness, but was inversely related to self-transcendence and spiritual well-being. *Quality*: Fair.

159. Koenig, H.G. 1992.   Religion and prevention of illness in later life.   In K. Pargament, K. Manton, & R. Hess (eds), Religion and Prevention in Mental Health NY: Haworth Press, pp 105-125.

Objective: Reviews research that examines the relationship between Judeo-Christian beliefs and behaviors and well-being in later life, and discusses to what extent religion's effects on mental health are transferred over to positive effects on physical health and use of health services.   *Sample & Methods*: Literature review and discussion. *Results & Conclusions*: Evidence is mounting to support a positive relationship between religious beliefs and activities and mental health in older adults. Because many persons turn to religion during a time of health crisis, the protective effects of religious beliefs and behaviors on physical health are more difficult to demonstrate. One exception is high blood pressure, which is usually not distressing enough to the person to stimulate a change in religious behaviors. Not surprisingly, numerous studies have demonstrated lower blood pressure in persons who are more religiously involved. Religion's effects on health care utilization are likewise complex. Because of its social aspects, religion may enhance appropriate health service use, whereas improved health may tend to decrease such use. Negative influences of religion on health are also discussed, and implications for health care providers and policy makers are provided.

160. Koenig, H.G. 1992.   Religion and mental health in later life.   In J.F. Schumacher (ed), Religion and Mental Health. London: Oxford Press, pp 177-188.

Objective: Examines the relationship between religious factors and mental health in older adults. *Sample & Methods*: Literature review and discussion. *Results & Conclusions*: Numerous studies conducted in different areas of the United States, Canada, and Great Britain have demonstrated positive correlations between religious beliefs and behaviors and mental health in both community-dwelling and clinical elderly populations. While "no association" findings are seldom published, the absence of any published literature demonstrating a inverse relationship between religious factors and mental health in later life is noteworthy.

161. Koenig, H.G. 1993. Judeo-Christian spirituality and mental
        health (editorial). Advances 9 (4):33-38.
Objective: Comments on David Aldridge's "Is there evidence for
spiritual healing?: A review and analysis." *Sample & Methods*: Review
of the literature and discussion. *Results & Conclusions*: The expression
"spirituality" can mean a lot of different things to a lot of different
people. Research in the United States that operationalizes spirituality
in terms of Judeo-Christian beliefs demonstrates abundant evidence for
healing, particularly in terms of emotional protection and healing.
These findings cannot be generalized to other religious belief systems
or to New Age spirituality, because there may be specific aspects of
Judeo-Christian belief (both interpersonal and person-Diety aspects)
which buffer against or facilitate the resolution of mental health
problems. The author challenges the notion that "physical healing" can
be proven by scientific methods, given the importance of "faith" in that
process.

162. Koenig, H.G. 1993. Religion and aging. Reviews in Clinical
        Gerontology 3(2): 195-203
Objective: Reviews recent research in the United States and Great
Britain on religion, aging, and health. *Sample & Methods*: Literature
review and discussion. *Results & Conclusions*: According to Gallup
Polls, the prevalence of belief in God and church attendance in the
United States has changed little over the past 50. In 1991, a George
Barna survey found that 89% of Americans agreed to the statement
'There is a God who watches over you and answers your prayers';
96% of persons over age 65 agreed to that statement. A number of
studies have demonstrated a relationship between religious beliefs or
practices and both physical and mental health. This paper briefly
summarizes the major studies, and explores social and public policy
implications. Illustrations and graphs included.

163. Koenig, H.G. 1993. Religion and hope in the disabled elder. In
        J. Levin (ed), Religious Factors in Aging and Health. Newbury
        Park, CA: Sage Publications, pp 18-52.
Objective: Examines the role that religion plays in maintaining hope in
older persons with disabling illnesses. *Sample & Methods*: Provides
two cases of older persons, one who is physically well, independent,
and "aging successfully", and one who is becoming progressively
disabled and struggling with desperate circumstances. *Results &
Conclusions*: Studies have shown that older persons with moderate to
severe physical disability who have strong religious beliefs are less

likely to become depressed. Judeo-Christian religious beliefs and behaviors, because of a positive underlying theology, provide older persons with hope and the possibility of happiness regardless of their external circumstances. Faith enables a person to transcend their circumstances and achieve a place of peace and contentment in the midst of turmoil.

164. Ellison, C.G., and L.K. George. 1994. Religious involvement, social ties, and social support in a Southeastern community. Journal for the Scientific Study of Religion 33:46-61.

Objective: Empirically examines the question of whether religious participation enhances the social resources of individuals. *Sample & Methods*: Random sample of 2,956 community-dwelling adults involved in Wave II of the Piedmont Health Survey (North Carolina), one of five sites of the National Institute of Mental Health Epidemiologic Catchment Area Program (cross-sectional study). Religious participation was measured by frequency of attendance at "church or other religious meetings". Social support was measured by the Duke Social Support Index that includes measures of frequency of inperson contacts, frequency of telephone contacts, received social support (variety of supports), and perceived quality of social relationships. Hierarchical regression was used to test a model of religion's relationship with social support. *Results*: Compared with infrequent church attenders, frequent attenders had larger social networks, more contacts with members of their social network, a greater variety of social supports, and a greater satisfaction with their social support (higher quality of support). These relationships remained significant after controlling for a wide range of sociodemographic and health variables. *Conclusions*: Future research is needed to further examine religious differences in social resources. *Quality*: Excellent. Provides a visual model (p 49) of religion's relationship to social support. This has important implications for research in this area: when assessing religion's relationship with health outcomes, a path model should be used to examine both the direct effects of religion on outcomes and its indirect effects through social support.

165. Koenig, H.G. 1995. Religion and the elderly. In M.S. Harper, B.D. Lebowitz, & R. Raschko (eds.), Community-based Mental Health Services/Behavioral Healthcare for the Elderly. Washington, D.C.: Federal Council on the Aging, DHHS, in press.

Objective: Examines issues related to religion's impact on the development and delivery of community-based mental health services for older adults. *Sample & Methods*: Literature review and discussion.

Results & Conclusions: Reviews special practices of selected religions, the impact of religion on the mental health of the elderly, and the use of and respect for religion in care and treatment. A state of the art review chapter and discussion sponsored by the National Institutes of Mental Health.

166. McFadden, S. 1995. Religion, spirituality, and aging. In J.E. Birren, K.W. Schiae (eds), Handbook of the Psychology of Aging (4th ed). San Diego: Academic Press, in press.
Objective: Examines the overall topic of religion, spirituality and aging. *Results & Conclusions*: A well-done, comprehensive review of the topic, including (1) examination of definitions of religion and spirituality, (2) discussion of the importance of religion in the lives of older adults (including ethnic minorities), (3) religious coping and its effects (positive and negative), (4) religious development in later life, (5) the effects of personality on religiousness, (6) the relationship between religiosity and mental health, and (7) the effects of cognitive impairment and dementia on religiousness and spirituality. *Quality*: Very Good. State of the art review.

RELIGION AND PHYSICAL HEALTH

Hypertension

167. Levin, J.S., and K.S. Markides. 1985. Religion and health in Mexican Americans. Journal of Religion and Health 24:60-69.
Objective: Examines the relationship between religiosity and measures of health, including blood pressure, in a sample of Mexican-Americans. *Sample & Methods*: The sample of 1125 was composed of three generations of predominantly Catholic, Mexican-Americans (San Antonio, Texas) of whom approximately one-third were men. *Results*: Church attendance was unrelated to blood pressure. Hypertension was more prevalent among older Mexican-Americans who rated themselves "highly religious" compared with those "less than very religious" (30%). For other findings related to health service utilization, see below. *Conclusions*: Higher blood pressures among the more religious may be due to increased guilt arising from pressures to conform to high behavioral standards. *Quality*: Good. The authors note in later review paper (Levin & Vanderpool 1989, ref #171, p 70) that this finding may be due to exclusion of the least religious subjects from the study because of mortality due to hypertension; furthermore, the onset of morbidity (stroke, heart failure, etc.) due to hypertension may have

caused persons to turn towards religion, creating a spurious association.

168. Department of Health and Human Services. 1987. Churches as an Avenue to High Blood Pressure Control. NIH Pub. No. 87-2725. Washington, DC: U.S. Government Printing Office.

Objective: Reviews the literature and encourages churches to take a more active effort in blood pressure control and prevention of stroke. *Sample & Methods*: Literature review & discussion. *Results & Conclusions*: The effects of religion on blood pressure may be explained by religiously sanctioned health-related behaviors, the stress-alleviating effects of religious worship, the positive psychodynamic effects of regular fellowship, and hereditary factors. Churches should be encouraged to engage in blood pressure screening, referral, tracking of compliance, education, and development of support groups. *Quality*: Good. The first government periodical advocating a cooperative effort between the church and the medical community in detecting, treating, and preventing health problems.

169. Beutler, J.J., J.T.M. Attevelt, S. Schouten, J.A.J. Faber, E.J.D. Mees, & G.G. Geijskes. 1988. Paranormal healing and hypertension. British Medical Journal 296:1491-1494

Objective: To experimentally assess the effects of healing by "laying on of hands" and healing by "thought projection" at a distance in a sample of patients with essential hypertension. *Sample & Methods*: This was a randomized, double-blind control trial in which 115 participants with hypertension (mean age 51) were randomly assigned to one of the two treatment groups or a placebo group. The treatment was performed once a week for 20 minutes in the morning for 15 weeks. *Results*: Overall, there was no significant difference in blood pressure change between the three groups. The group receiving the "laying on of hands" experienced a significant increase of diastolic BP immediately after onset of the procedure (1.8 mm, $p < .05$). When well-being was assessed at the end of the study, 83% of those in the "laying on of hands" group reported improvement in well-being, compared with 43% of subjects in the "thought projection" group and 41% of controls. *Conclusions*: Laying on of hands did not produce greater decreases of blood pressure than did thought projection or no treatment; nevertheless, it was associated with greater well-being. *Quality*: Very good. Unlike Byrd's 1988 study below, this investigation did not assess the effects of Judeo-Christian prayer or healing; instead, it examined the effects of non-religious paranormal healing methods.

170. Larson, D.B., H.G. Koenig, B.H. Kaplan, R.F. Greenberg, E. Logue, & H.A. Tyroler. 1989. The impact of religion on blood pressure status in men. Journal of Religion and Health 28:265-278.

Objective: Examines the relationship between blood pressure, importance of religion, and church attendance. *Sample & Methods*: In a community survey of 407 men, participants were asked about importance of religion and frequency of church attendance; in addition, systolic and diastolic blood pressures were measured and weight-height ratio (Quetelet Index), socioeconomic status, and smoking habits were determined. *Results*: Diastolic blood pressures of men with high church attendance and high religious importance were significantly lower than those of men in the low importance, low attendance group; these differences persisted after adjusting for the effects of other variables described above. Among men age 55 or over, the difference in mean diastolic blood pressure was both statistically and clinically significant (6 mm of mercury). *Conclusions*: Both religious attitudes and involvement may interact favorably in their effects on blood pressure in men. *Quality*: Very good. Provides more recent confirmation of earlier findings.

171. Levin, J.S., and H.Y. Vanderpool. 1989. Is religion therapeutically significant for hypertension? Social Sciences and Medicine 29:69-78.

Objective: Comprehensively reviews the research evidence for a link between religious beliefs and activities and a lowered risk for high blood pressure. *Sample & Methods*: Literature review and discussion. *Results & Conclusions*: Religious commitment is inversely related to blood pressure; several religious groups have relatively low rates of hypertension-related illness. The authors posit 12 possible explanations for this link, including the promotion of health-related behavior, genetic predispositions in some groups, and positive psychological effects of religious behaviors and belief systems. Superempirical influences are also discussed.

Quality: Very good. Superb literature review.

See also:

8. Koenig et al. 1988. Journal of the American Geriatrics Society 36:362-374.

Heart Disease and Stroke

172. Byrd, R.C. 1988. Positive therapeutic effects of intercessory prayer in a coronary care unit population. Southern Medical Journal 81:826-829.
Objective: To examine the effects of intercessory prayer in a coronary care unit (CCU) population on patient outcomes. *Sample & Methods*: Over a 10 month period, 393 patients (mean age 58) admitted to San Francisco General Hospital CCU were randomized to either an intercessory prayer group (n = 192) or a control group (n = 201). Patients were unaware that they were being prayed for. *Results*: Multivariate analysis revealed a significant difference (p < .0001) between prayed for patients and control patients in number of negative events happening to patients after study entry (ventilatory support, antibiotics, diuretics); furthermore, after categorizing patients into "good", "intermediate", and "bad" outcomes, it was found that prayer group members had 85% good, 1% intermediate, and 14% bad results, whereas control patients had 73% good, 5% intermediate and 22% bad outcomes (p < .01). *Conclusions*: Prayer works! *Quality*: Good; a most remarkable study that has received much praise and much condemnation by various groups; has not yet been replicated, although studies are currently ongoing.

173. Levin, J.S., C.D. Jenkins, and R.M. Rose. 1988. Religion, Type A behavior, and health. Journal of Religion and Health 27 (4):267-278.
Objective: Examines the effects of religion on the relationships between Type A behavior and health. *Sample & Methods*: Prospective three-year study of 408 male air traffic controllers (New York and New England) surveyed in 1973-1978; average age was 32 years and length of experience 11 years. Jenkins Activity Survey (JAS) measured degree of Type A behavior. *Results*: JAS scores were lowest in Protestant frequent church attenders and highest in Catholic infrequent attenders and atheists/agnostics. The relationship between JAS and physical illness was strongest among Protestant infrequent attenders, atheists/agnostics, and recent converts; it was lowest among Catholic frequent attenders. The inverse relationships between JAS and both diastolic and systolic blood pressure were strongest in atheists or agnostics; in other words, in this group Type A behavior was associated with **lower** blood pressures. The relationship between JAS and subjective distress was strongest in Catholic frequent attenders and persons with stable affiliations. The relationship between JAS and alcohol consumption was strongest in Protestant infrequent attenders and lowest in Catholic frequent attenders. *Conclusions*: Type A

behavior is more likely to have deleterious effects on health and drive alcohol consumption among Protestant infrequent attenders, atheists/agnostics, and recent converts; on the other hand, Type A behavior is associated with lower blood pressures in persons with weak or no religious ties. *Quality*: Excellent. Unique study. This study has relevance to older age groups since Type A behavior predisposes to heart disease, the most common cause of death in the elderly. Dr. Bert H. Kaplan has also written extensively on this subject (Department of Epidemiology, School of Public health, CB# 7400, McGavran-Greenberg Hall, University of North Carolina at Chapel Hill, NC 27599).

174. Colantonio, A., S.V. Kasl, and A.M. Ostfeld. 1992. Depressive symptoms and other psychosocial factors as predictors of stroke in the elderly. American Journal of Epidemiology 136: 884-894.

Objective: Examines psychosocial variables (including religiousness) as baseline risk factors for the development of stroke over time in community-dwelling older adults. *Sample & Methods*: Prospective longitudinal study of 2,812 adults age 65 or over in New Haven, Connecticut (same cohort studied by Idler). Incidence of stroke was monitored between 1982 (when baseline data collected) until 1988. Univariate Cox regression analysis was utilized to assess predictive ability of baseline variables. *Results & Conclusions*: Both high depression scores (CESD) ($p < .05$) and infrequent church attendance ($p < .001$) predicted high stroke incidence. Stroke incidence among persons who never attended church was almost double that of those who attended church weekly or more often (8.6% vs 4.7%). When combined with other significant predictor variables (age, sex, hypertension, diabetes, physical function, and smoking, the relationships with depression and church attendance lost their significance [this, however, does not eliminate the possibility that frequent church attendance may have reduced the likelihood of stroke indirectly through its impact on these other predictors variables]. *Quality*: Very good.

Cancer

175. Yates, J., B. Chalmer, P. St. James, M. Follansbee, and F. McKegney. 1981. Religion in patients with advanced cancer. Medical and Pediatric Oncology 9:121-128.

Objective: Examines relationships between religious belief, activity and connections, with ratings of happiness, life satisfaction, and pain level. *Sample & Methods*: Questionnaire administered to 71 patients with a projected survival of 3 to 12 months, as part of the Cancer Care and Rehabilitation Project at Vermont Regional Cancer Center in Burlington; sample characteristics included female (61%), mean age (59 years), cancer location (lung 31%, breast 25%, gastrointestinal 15%, other 28%), and religious affiliation (Catholic 39%, Protestant 45%, Jewish 3%, none 13%). Religious beliefs, church affiliation, importance of church, attendance at services, and closeness to God were religious variables measured. *Results*: 92% agreed that God exists, 83% believed in God as a personal being, 80% agreed that prayer was helpful, half said that church or religion was very important in their lives, and two-thirds said that they had felt close to God or nature in the past few weeks. Religious beliefs were positively correlated with life satisfaction ($r = 0.41$, $p < .005$), as was church affiliation ($r = .25$, $p < .05$), importance of church ($r = 0.31$, $p < .005$), attendance at services ($r = 0.35$, $p < .005$), and closeness to God ($r = 0.33$, $p < .005$). Church affiliation and church attendance were also associated with "happiness"; importance of church, attendance at services, and closeness to God were all correlated with "positive affect." Pain level was inversely correlated with religious belief ($r = -.29$, $p < .01$), church affiliation ($r = -.22$, $p < .05$), importance of church ($r = -.33$, $p < .005$), church attendance ($r = -.24$, $p < .05$) and closeness to God ($r = -.25$, $p < .05$). *Conclusions*: Religion provided an important source of support for these patients. Religious belief changed little over time, and was not related to survival. *Quality*: Very good.

176. Mayberry, J.F. 1982. Epidemiological studies of gastrointestinal cancer in Christian sects. Journal of Clinical Gastroenterology 4:115-1121.

Objective: Reviews studies examining rates of cancer in a number of religious groups, focusing on the role of lifestyle and diet as it affects the risk of developing gastrointestinal cancer. *Sample & Method*: Literature review and discussion. *Results*: Studies show both increased and decreased rates of colon cancer in older Catholic nuns; lower rates of gastric cancer in Lutheran Clergymen, although higher rates of pancreatic cancer; lower rates of colon cancer in Adventists; lower rates of colon cancer in Mormon men. *Conclusions*: Associations between gastrointestinal cancers and religious group may help to explain the role of diet in the etiology of these cancers. *Quality*: Good review; documents the effects that religion can have on health - even if only through diet and healthy life styles.

177. Acklin, M., E. Brown, P. Mauger. 1983. The role of religious values in coping with cancer. Journal of Religion and Health 22:322-333.

Objective: Tests the hypothesis that intrinsic religious values and life meaning enhance adjustment and well-being in patients with cancer. Sample & Methods: 44 adult medical patients in Atlanta, Georgia: 26 with cancer (mean age 48, 77% women), 18 with physical illness but not cancer (mean age 42). *Results*: Intrinsic religiosity and transcendent meaning were slightly lower in those with cancer compared with non-cancer patients. Among cancer patients, transcendent meaning was inversely related to despair (-.57, p<.0001), anger/hostility (-.50, p<.01), and social isolation (-.60, p<.0001); intrinsic religiosity was inversely related to all psychological measures, but was statistically significant only for anger/hostility (-.34, p<.05). Frequency of church attendance was inversely related both to anger/hostility (-.39, p<.05) and to social isolation (-.32, p<.05). *Conclusions*: Religious values, meaning, and images can be utilized to help support cancer patients to develop "broader, sustaining felt connections with larger horizons of life beyond the self." *Quality*: Good.

178. Phillips, R.L., and D.A. Snowden. 1983. Association of meat and coffee use with cancers of the large bowel, breast, and prostate among Seventh-Day Adventists: Preliminary results. Cancer Research 43(Suppl):2403-2408.
Objective: Compares mortality rates from cancers of the large bowel, breast, and prostate between 7th-Day Adventists and non-Adventists. *Sample & Methods*: Death rate from non-smoking related cancer over a 21-year period was examined among 21,295 white Adventists in California, and was compared to the rate among 112,726 non-Adventists. *Results*: The age-sex-adjusted morality rates per 100,000 persons for large bowel cancer (32.6 vs 50.6), for breast cancer (63.4 vs 74.7), and for prostate cancer (34.7 vs 40.0) were substantially lower among Adventists. The lower rate of large bowel cancer within the Adventist group was unrelated to meat use. *Conclusions*: Further studies are needed to help explain the relatively large difference in colon cancer rates between Adventists and non-Adventists that cannot be explained by low meat use among Adventists. *Quality*: Good. Also see: Phillips, R.L., J.W. Kuzma, W.L. Beeson, et al. 1980. Influence of selection versus lifestyle on risk of fatal cancer and cardiovascular disease among Seventh-Day Adventists. American Journal of Epidemiology 112:296-314; Baider, L., and M. Sarell. 1983. Perceptions and causal attributions of Israeli women with breast cancer concerning their illness: The effects of ethnicity and religiosity. Psychotherapy and Psychosomatics 39:136-143 [Israeli breast cancer patients holding fatalistic religious attitudes toward their illness coped less well than those who had more scientific-oriented beliefs about

their disease, although this finding may have been founded by European background]; and Tryoyer, H. 1988. Review of cancer among four religious sects: Evidence that life-styles are distinctive sets of risk factors. Social Science and Medicine 26:1007-1017 [Amish found to have relatively low rates of cervical cancer, due to strong prohibitions against extra-marital or pre-marital sex].

179.   Mitchell-Beren, M.E., M.E. Dodds, K.L. Choi, and T.R. Waskerwitz. 1989. A colorectal cancer prevention, screening, and evaluation program in community black churches. CA-A Cancer Journal for Clinicians 39:115-118.

Objective: Describes a secondary prevention program for cancer in Black churches that involves educational and screening interventions for colorectal cancer. *Results & Conclusions*: Prevention of cancer mortality has been largely a result of secondary prevention programs. For physical illnesses like colon cancer and hypertension which have a high prevalence in elderly Blacks, the church would seem an ideal place to coordinate and organize such screening efforts. *Quality*: Very good. Also see: Eng, E., J. Hatch, and A. Callan. 1985. Institutionalizing social support through the church and into the community. Health Education Quarterly 12:81-92 [describes a program in North Carolina where church members are trained as "health advisors" who are then responsible for organizing health fairs, screening programs, facilitating self-help groups, and teaching about weight reduction and stress management. Given that the majority of elderly persons attend church at least weekly, this would seem the ideal setting for such health promotion activities to take place].

180.   Spiegel, D., J.R. Bloom, H.C. Kraemer, E. Gottheil. 1989. Effect of psychosocial treatment on survival of patients with metastatic breast cancer. Lancet (No. 8668):888-891.

Objective: Examines the effect of psychosocial intervention on the survival of patients with metastatic breast cancer. *Sample and Methods*: 86 patients with metastatic breast cancer were randomly allocated either to an intervention group (n = 50), where they received 1 year of weekly supportive group therapy with self-hypnosis for pain, or a control group which was assigned to routine oncological care (n = 36). Time of survival was compared between the two groups at 10 years. *Results*: Survival was significantly longer for patients in the supportive group therapy intervention (36.6 months vs 18.9 months, p < .0001); these results persisted after controlling for other risk factors know to affect survival. *Conclusions*: Social support is an important factor in survival; furthermore, involvement in a group may allow patients to mobilize their resources better, comply better with medical treatments, and perhaps improved appetite and diet due to less depression. *Quality*: Excellent. It is easy to extrapolate these results to the potentially positive effects of church membership and participation on the health of older adults (who may otherwise be isolated and without such support).

181. Dwyer, J.W., L.L. Clarke, and M.K. Miller. 1990. The effect of religious concentration and affiliation on county cancer mortality rates. Journal of Health and Social Behavior 31:185-202.
Objective: Examines the effect of religious concentration and religious affiliation on cancer mortality rates. *Sample & Methods*: County cancer mortality rates were determined using National Center for Health Statistics standardized data. Church membership and denomination were taken from a separate study that examined these variables at the county level. Other national data bases were used to obtain information on cancer risk factors. Structural equation modeling (LISREL) was used to analyze the data. *Results*: Conservative Protestants had lower rates of cancer mortality than liberal Protestants. Counties with higher concentrations of conservative or moderate Protestants had significantly lower cancer mortality than those with higher concentrations of liberal Protestants. Likewise, counties with higher concentrations of Jewish persons had the highest rates of cancer mortality, whereas areas with high concentrations of Mormons, had the lowest mortality rates. *Conclusions*: The findings suggest that religion has a significant impact on mortality rates for all malignancies combined, digestive cancer, and respiratory cancer; the results persist after controlling for demographic, environmental, and regional factors known to affect cancer mortality. These results are attributed mostly to religion's effects as a social structure which diminishes one's exposure to (or causes social disapproval of) unhealthy behaviors associated with cancer. *Quality*: Excellent. Also see: Seeman, T.E., G.A. Kaplan, L. Knudsen, R. Cohen, and J. Guralnik. 1987. Social network ties and mortality among the elderly in the Alameda County study. American Journal of Epidemiology 126:714-723 [microlevel church participation may affect cancer risk].

See also:

8. Koenig et al. 1988. Journal of the American Geriatrics Society 36:362-374.

Mortality

182. King, H., and F.B. Locke. 1980. American white Protestant clergy as a low-risk population for mortality research. Journal of the National Cancer Institute 65:1115-1124.
Objective: Compares mortality rates between U.S. white clergy and total U.S. males with work experience. *Sample & Methods*: 28,124 clergymen in five predominantly white Protestant denominations (American Baptists, United Lutherans, Episcopalians, United Presbyterians, and the Lutheran-Missouri Synod). *Results*: For this group, 7,243 deaths would be expected during a 10 year period, based on mortality rates for white males in the general population; instead, only 5,207 deaths were observed (SMR 72); note that physicians had an SMR of 90. Lower mortality among clergy was attributed to a lower risk of cancer (SMR 63), especially lung (SMR 35), stomach (SMR 48), rectum (SMR 51), and bladder (SMR 56) cancers. Likewise, deaths due to cardiovascular and renal disorders (67% of all deaths) were less frequent among clergy (SMR 74). The strongest effects were seen at younger ages, and diminished with age. *Conclusions*: The extremely low mortality of white male clergy requires more intensive investigations; this protective effect apparently decreases with age. *Quality*: Good.

183. Zuckerman, D.M., S.V. Kasl, and A.M. Ostfeld. 1984. Psychosocial predictors of mortality among the elderly poor. American Journal of Epidemiology 119:410-423.
Objective: Examines the role of religion, well-being, and social contacts as predictors of mortality. *Sample & Methods*: Sample consisted of 400 persons age 62 or older in New Haven, CT; 225 were forced to move from their homes because of urban renewal, eviction, or condemned housing and extreme financial hardships; 173 additional elders from the same neighborhoods were selected to act as controls. During 90 minute interviews, data were collected on sociodemographics, health status, social contacts, psychological state, and religiousness (attendance at religious services, religiousness, religion as a source of strength). Mortality during a 2-year followup was examined and correlated with predictors. *Results*: Religiousness had a protective effect, but only among the elderly in poorer health; this occurred despite the fact that religiousness and health status were virtually independent of each other in this sample. The non-religious elderly in poor health were almost two and one-half times (OR 2.32) more likely to die than the religious elderly in poor health. Strength from religion was the strongest predictor of the three religious variables, and church attendance was the weakest predictor.

Conclusions: Religiousness appears to have a protective effect against mortality among the elderly poor with health problems. *Quality*: Very good.

184.   Seeman, T.E., G.A. Kaplan, L. Knudsen, R. Cohen, and J. Guralnik. 1987. Social network ties and mortality among the elderly in the Alameda County Study. American Journal of Epidemiology 126:714-723.

Objective: To examine the relative importance of social ties as predictors of 17-year survival for Alameda County Study participants. *Sample & Methods*: Participants (n = 4174) were placed into three groups based on age at study initiation in 1965 (ages 38-49, 50-59, 60-69, and 70 or over). Survival was determined by Cox proportional hazards models for each age group; examined were the effects on survival of marital status, social isolation, church membership, and membership in other groups, controlled for age, sex, race, and baseline health status. *Results*: Membership in church groups was associated with decreased mortality risk in all age groups (except ages 50-59), whereas membership in other types of social groups was generally not significantly related to morality risk. Social isolation (measured by contacts with close friends and/or relatives) was the only other measure of social ties that predicted survival. *Conclusions*: Compared with other forms of social ties, church membership is among the strongest predictors of survival for persons age 60 or over. This effect may be partly mediated by smoking status and level of depression. *Quality*: Very good.

185.   Idler, E.L. 1994. Religion, health, and nonphysical senses of self. Paper presented at the annual meeting of the Southern Sociological Society in Raleigh, North Carolina (April, 1994).

Objective: Tests two hypotheses about the relationship between religion and health - first, that higher levels of religiousness may be associated with poorer health as people in the midst of crisis turn to religion for comfort and social support; second, that self-ratings of health represent broad conceptualizations of self in which physical abilities are de-emphasized and religious or spiritual self-identities are stressed. *Sample & Methods*: Random cross-sectional sample of 146 disabled patients attending an urban rehabilitation clinic (Rutgers University). Physical health was measured in the following manner. Disability was objectively assessed by physician examination using the musculoskeletal exam portion of the National Health and Nutrition Examination Survey (NHANES-I). A health status questionnaire assessed pain, stiffness, and swelling in joints, as well as the presence of chronic health conditions associated with increased mortality.

Psychosocial variables measured included general activities, social support, depression, neuroticism, optimism, general well-being, body consciousness, religious activities and help sought from religion, and physical/nonphysical sense of self. Dependent variables in the analysis were perceived disability assessed using a 10-item physical activities of daily living scale, and self-rated health measured by a single item. *Results*: When asked whether religious beliefs helped patients with their health problems, 62% responded affirmatively. Multivariate analyses found that seeking help from religion was associated with greater disability. Disabled persons also had a greater nonphysical sense of self than did non-disabled persons; including the latter variable in the model reduced but did not eliminate the association between disability and help sought from religion. Thus for disability, both hypotheses were confirmed. For self-rated health, however, neither hypothesis was supported. *Conclusions*: Disabled persons frequently turn to religion for help; one of the ways religion helps is by allowing them to "rise above" their problems by putting them in a context in which one's own physical body doesn't matter that much (enhances nonphysical sense of self). *Quality*: Very good.

186. Koenig, H.G. 1994. Use of acute hospital services and mortality among religious and non-religious copers with medical illness. Journal of Religious Gerontology, in submission.

Objective: Examines the effects of religious coping on survival and use of health services. *Sample & Methods*: 161 men under age 40 and 850 men over age 65 consecutively admitted to the medical and neurological inpatient services of a VA medical center were questioned about religious coping. Twelve younger (8%) and 85 older (10%) men were classified as strong religious copers; 36 younger (22%) and 129 older (15%) men were classified as non-religious copers. Religious (RCs) and non-religious copers (NRCs) were followed up for 0 to 32 months after hospital discharge, comparing number of hospitalizations, total days hospitalized, compliance with clinic visits, and morality rate. *Results*: The average number of hospital admissions and days hospitalized was significantly lower for RC's than for NRC's; these difference, however, were entirely due to the fact that non-religious copers were more likely than religious copers to be lost to followup. Non-religious copers were more likely than religious copers to be "no-shows" at followup clinic visits. Mortality rate during the 14 month average followup period was 25% for religious copers and 23% for non-religious copers, a non-significant difference. *Conclusions*: Short-term followup of physically ill hospitalized men found no differences in healthcare service use or mortality between religious and non-religious copers. Long-term followup of this cohort is needed.

See also:

129. Idler, E.L., and S.V. Kasl. 1992. American Journal of Sociology
     97:1052-1079.

General Health

187. Levin, J.S., and K.S. Markides. 1986. Religious attendance and
     subjective health. Journal for the Scientific Study of Religion
     25:31-40.
Objective: The authors examine the relationship between church attendance and subjective health. *Sample & Methods*: 1125 Mexican Americans (375 each in younger, middle, and elderly generations) were surveyed in San Antonio, TX in 1981-82; two-thirds of sample were women; all subjects were Catholics. *Results*: A positive association was found between attendance and subjective health among young and older generations of female participants only; this association persisted even after controlling for non-religious social participation, suggesting that the relationship could not be explained entirely in terms of the positive effects of social interaction. However, when self-perceived "physical capacity" was controlled for, the relationship between attendance and health became non-significant. *Conclusions*: Religious effects of church attendance on health are not solely a proxy for social support; rather, the physical capacity to attend church largely explains this association. *Quality*: Good; note, however, that "physical capacity" was based on the item "About how much of the time does bad health, sickness or pain stop you from doing things you'd like to be doing?" Subjective health was strongly correlated with this item (+ .45 in elders and + .41 in younger); one might argue that these two variables could have been used interchangeably as a measure of health; controlling for either one in the analysis, then, would account for most of the variance in the other variable, diminishing positive correlations with other variables (like church attendance).

188. Levin, J.S., and P.L. Schiller. 1987. Is there a religious factor in
     health. Journal of Religion and Health 26:9-36.
Objective: Reviews epidemiologic studies examining the relationship between religion and health. *Sample & Method*: Over 200 studies are reviewed in nine health-related areas: cardiovascular disease, hypertension and stroke, gastrointestinal illness, general health, mortality, cervical and uterine cancer, all other cancers, cancer in India, and health of the clergy. Theoretical, methodological, and future research issues are also addressed. *Results & Conclusions*: Many

studies have obtained positive association between religion and health, providing "overwhelming evidence" that such a relationship exists. The authors explain that religious faith might reduce fear and provide comfort when stress occurs, thus acting indirectly through the central nervous system to decrease the risk of illness and mortality. *Quality*: Very good. The most comprehensive review of the topic to date.

189. Hogstel, M.O., and M. Kashka. 1989. Staying healthy after age 85. Geriatric Nursing, Jan/Feb issue: 16-18.
Objective: Examines accounts by the old-old on how they maintain their health and well-being. *Sample & Methods*: A convenience sample of 302 persons over age 85 from nursing homes (30%), retirement centers (25%), private homes (25%), hospitals (12%), and senior centers (8%) were interviewed 15 min to 2 hrs. Mean age of the sample was 89 years, 74% were women, 95% white, 85% from a metropolitan area, 83% regular church attenders). The structured interview collected information on demographics and family composition, health problems, and included the Lifelong Health Practices Scale. *Results*: Secrets to a long life were the following (in order of most frequent mention): (1) activity (hard work, exercise, keeping physically and mentally active), (2) strong belief in God and Christian living, (3) positive attitude toward self and others, (4) living a clean life (no alcohol, drugs, or smoking), and (5) good nutrition. Conclusions: Faith in God and Christian living rank right up there among the factors that the old-old feel contribute to their longevity and health. *Quality*: Very good. This is the most rapidly growing age group in the United States, yet very little information is known about the key elements that account for survival.

190. Ferraro, K.F., and C.M. Albrecht-Jensen. 1991. Does religion influence adult health? Journal for the Scientific Study of Religion 30:193-202.
Objective: Examines the associations between religious affiliation, practice, and subjective health status. *Sample & Methods*: National sample of 1473 persons age 18 or older interviewed during the 1984 and 1987 General Social Surveys (NORC). *Results*: Health status was inversely related to age and conservative religious affiliation, but positively related to white race, higher income, higher education, employment status, and religious practice. Four reasons are offered to explain the negative association between health and conservative religious affiliation, including resistance to medical intervention, fatalistic views of illness, fewer health protective behaviors, and less knowledge about medical interventions. A positive relationship was found between age and both religious practice and "closeness to God".

Conclusions: Religion can have both positive and negative associations with health, depending on what measure of religion is used. The association between religiosity and age may be due to the selective survival of the most religious persons (see Moberg, D.O. 1990. Religion and aging. In Ferraro, KF (ed), <u>Gerontology: Perspectives and Issues</u>, 179-205. New York: Springer). *Quality*: Very good.

191. Levin, J.S., and H.Y. Vanderpool. 1992. Religious factors in physical health and the prevention of illness. In Pargament, K.I., Maton, K.I., Hess, R.E. (Eds), <u>Religion and Prevention in Mental Health: Research, Vision, and Action</u>. NY: Haworth Press, pp 83-103.

Objective: Reviews the literature linking religious background, beliefs, behaviors, and commitment to medical illnesses, emphasizing the role of religion in disease prevention and health maintenance. *Sample & Methods*: Literature review and discussion. *Results & Conclusions*: A wealth of studies exist (over 300) which demonstrate a link between religion and health; given this association, recommendations are made on how religious organizations may work with community agencies to maximize health. Special attention is given to disease prevention and health promotion in older adults, and the role churches can play. *Quality*: Very good. A comprehensive, concise, and balanced review.

192. Ferraro, K.F. 1994. Firm believers? Religion, body weight, and well-being. Paper presented at the annual meeting of the Southern Sociological Society, April, Raleigh, NC.

Objective: Examines relationships between religion and body weight, and the effects of each on well-being. *Sample & Methods*: Data came from two sources: (1) U.S. ecological data on prevalence of obesity for each state and its relationship with religion, and (2) first wave of Americans' Changing Lives, a national survey of 3,617 community-dwelling adults. Well-being measured by a single item assessing happiness and by an 11-item version of the CES-D. Religious measures included church attendance, religious book reading, watching or listening to religious TV or radio, religious importance, religious coping, and religious affiliation. *Results*: Highest body weight (by Quetelet index) was found among pietistic and fundamentalist Protestants, while Jewish and non-Christian affiliations had the lowest body weight; these differences disappeared when controlled for social class, ethnicity, and marital status. When obese and slight persons were compared on other measures of religiosity, obesity was associated with higher levels of religiosity. Obese persons were also less happy, more depressed, and less satisfied than thin persons. Frequency of church attendance, however, counterbalanced the negative effects of obesity on well-being. *Conclusions*: Obese persons are more likely to be religious and to be unhappy; however, if they attend church frequently, this counterbalances the negative effects of obesity on well-being. *Quality*: Very good. Novel findings. Also has implications for overweight elderly persons.

193. Koenig, H.G. 1995. Religion and health in later life. In M. Kimble, S.H. McFadden, J.W. Ellor, & J.J. Seeber (eds), Aging, Religion, and Spirituality: A Handbook. Minneapolis: Fortress Press, in press.

Objective: Reviews the literature linking religious factors with mental and physical health in later life. *Sample & Methods*: Literature review and discussion. *Results & Conclusions*: Religious factors are involved in the physical, emotional, and social well-being of older adults. Religion exerts its effects over the lifetime of the individual, as well as more immediately in later life. Religion and spirituality are two different concepts that need to be kept separate, particularly when generalizing results from research that measures one or the other.

Health Care Utilization

194. Schiller PL, Levin JS (1988). Is there a religious factor in health care utilization?: A review. Social Science in Medicine 27:1369-1379.

Objective: To perform a comprehensive literature review on the topic and to report the results of a study of their own on religiosity and health service use. *Sample & Methods*: 909 adults in West Virginia comprised the sample for this report. Religious variables were denominational affiliation, church attendance, and holding a church office. Health service use (time since last hospitalization, length of hospital stay, and physician visits) was determined by subject recall. *Results & Discussion*: After controlling for age, sex, race, education, health status, chronic diseases, and health locus of control, subjects holding a church office had both shorter lengths of hospital stay and longer time since last hospitalization ($p < .01$). Religious affiliation and church attendance were unrelated to either of these service variables. *Conclusions*: Results are suggestive that involvement in the church at the officer level may reduce health service use, although direction of causation is difficult to determine because of the cross-sectional nature of the data. The authors call for further research in this area. *Quality*: Very good.

(167.) Levin JS, Markides KS (1985). Religion and health in Mexican
        Americans. Journal of Religion and Health 24:60-69.
        [**Reviewed previously.**]
Objective: Among the objectives of this study was to examine the
relationship between religious attendance, self-rated religiosity, days of
bed disability, and physician visits per year. *Sample & Methods*: The
sample of 1125 was composed of three generations of predominantly
Catholic, Mexican-Americans (San Antonio, Texas) of whom
approximately one-third were men. Bed disability was defined as
number of days spent in bed the previous year because of sickness or
injury and was determined by retrospective self-report. Physician visits
were obtained by the same method. *Results*: Overall, they found no
significant relationship between religious attendance and either days of
bed disability or number of physician visits. However, in a subgroup
of men aged 65 to 80, there was a trend towards fewer disability days
and fewer physician visits for frequent church attenders. On the other
hand, they found that bed disability days more frequent in men aged
40 to 65 who rated themselves more highly religious (self-rated
religiosity) and a similar, though non-significant, trend emerged for
number of physician visits. Thus, the only statistically significant
finding in this study was an increase in healthcare utilization with
increasing self-rated religiosity. *Conclusions*: The results of this study
provide little evidence for the hypothesis that religious attendance or
religiosity reduces use of health services among older Mexican-
Americans. *Quality*: Good.

See also:

186. Koenig, H.G. 1994. Use of acute hospital services and mortality
      among religious and non-religious copers with medical illness.
      Journal of Religious Gerontology, in submission.

Part III

Practical Applications of Research Findings

APPLICATIONS IN CLINICAL POPULATIONS

Medical

195. Weikart, R. 1986. Cooperation between clergy and family practice physicians: A new area of ministry. <u>Journal of Pastoral Care</u> 40(2):151-157.

Objective: Describes an experimental program to determine the impact of meetings between clergy and physicians on referral patterns and delivery of holistic care. *Sample & Methods*: Informal breakfast meetings were held between 8-10 clergy and 4-6 family physicians for mutual education and dialogue. Out of these meetings came a series of 11 seminars on psychosocial and counseling issues attended jointly by physicians and clergy; to assess the effectiveness of this joint training, clergy were divided into experimental (n = 6) and control (n = 6) groups. Referral patterns were examined before and after the seminar series. *Results*: In the year before the seminar series, clergy referred 6 people to family physicians; in the year after the course, clergy referred 58 persons to the physicians. Control clergy referred 8 people to physicians during the year before the course, but only 3 people in the year after the course. Family physicians referred no patients to clergy during the year before the course, but 8 persons during the year after the seminar series. Patients referred either to physicians or to clergy reported extreme satisfaction with the physician/clergy interaction. *Conclusions*: A relatively brief joint-educational program may contribute to improvements in clergy-physician relationships, as well as referral tendencies and improved overall patient care. *Quality*:

Good. Study has direct applicability to care for the elderly, given that most of the mental health care of this group will be provided by primary care physicians who may need help from clergy, especially in the counseling arena.

196. Koenig, H.G., and J. Seeber. 1987. Religion, spirituality, and
      aging. Journal of the American Geriatrics Society 35:472.
Objective: To expose geriatric physicians to a recent conference on Religion, Spirituality, and Aging sponsored by the American Society on Aging and National Interfaith Coalition on Aging. *Sample & Methods*: Discussion. *Results & Conclusions*: Health care professionals need to be aware of important developments in social gerontology to more effectively meet the social and psychological needs of older adults; religious resources may be utilized to help meet these needs. Demonstrates a growing recognition by professionals of the importance of this area.

197. Kuhn, C.C. 1988. A spiritual inventory of the medically ill
      patient. Psychiatric Medicine 6:87-100.
Objective: Advances the concept of spirituality as a legitimate and purposeful area of medical inquiry, and proposes specific measures by which physicians can assess spiritual health or illness. *Sample & Methods*: Review and discussion. *Results & Conclusions*: Provides a historical background and presents a spiritual inventory that explores meaning and purpose, belief and faith, love, forgiveness, prayer, capacity for quiet and meditation, and worship. *Quality*: Very Good; practical for the clinician, and applicable to older patients.

198. Koenig, H.G., L.B. Bearon, and R. Dayringer. 1989. Physician
      perspectives on the role of religion in the physician-older
      patient relationship. Journal of Family Practice 28:441-448.
Objective: Examines beliefs of family physicians and general practitioners concerning the importance and impact of religion in the lives of their older patients. *Sample & Methods*: Surveyed a random sample of 160 Illinois physicians, asking whether or not they thought religion had positive or negative effects on health, whether religious issues should be addressed during a medical visit, how such issues should be discussed, whether physicians should pray with patients and if they ever did. *Results*: Nearly two-thirds of physicians felt that prayer with patients was appropriate under certain circumstances, and one-third indicated they had prayed with patients. The strongest predictors of physicians' belief in the appropriateness of addressing religious concerns were two attitudinal variables which indicated an understanding of the importance of religion to older adults.

Conclusions: Beliefs and attitudes of the physician are important factors in determining both the receptivity to discussion of religious issues and the likelihood that patients will mention them. [This article received the 1991 Commission on Ministries in Special Settings (COMMIS) Research Award.]

See also:

8. Koenig et al. 1988. Journal of the American Geriatrics Society 36:362-374.

Nursing

199. Fish, S., and J.A. Shelly. 1983. Spiritual Care: The Nurses Role. Downers Grove, Ill: InterVarsity Press.
Objective: Among other things, defines spiritual needs of patients and examines how to best meet them. *Sample & Methods*: Contains several spiritual needs research studies of hospitalized patients (all ages), including a discussion of assessment instruments. *Results & Conclusions*: Contains chapters on "responsible nursing", "what is human", "what are spiritual needs", "use of prayer", "use of scripture", "when to refer to clergy", and so forth. *Quality*: Very good; a practical text for nurses; very applicable to the care of older adults with chronic illness. Contains compiled data from 10 years of surveys and seminars.

200. Gress, L.D., and R.T. Bahr. 1984. Spiritual changes of aging. In Gress LD, Bahr RT (eds), The Aging Person: A Holistic Perspective. St. Louis: CV Mosby, pp 82-91.
Objective: Examines spiritual changes that occur with aging. *Method*: Review and theoretical discussion, depending heavily on the writings of Jourard, Jung, Sinnott, Kas, and others. *Results & Conclusions*: Explores the meaning of spirituality in later life, discusses spiritual growth and development, and provides challenges to the older person and their caregiver in this area. *Quality*: Fair; interesting references.

201. Granstrom, S.L. 1985. Spiritual nursing care for oncology patients. Topics in Clinical Nursing, April issue, pp 39-45.
Objective: Examines spiritual issues that nurses should consider when caring for patients with cancer, and the problems that may be encountered. *Sample & Method*: Discussion. *Results & Conclusions*: Nurses must deal with (1) pluralism, (2) fear, (3) their own spiritual quest, (4) confusion over difference between religious and spiritual

concerns, and (5) their attitudes toward aging. *Quality*: Fair; deals with spirituality in a very broad context. Somewhat unique, however, in addressing spiritual needs of cancer patients.

202. Hungelmann, J., E. Kenkel-Rossi, L. Klassen, and R. Stollenwerk. 1985. Spiritual well-being in older adults: Harmonious interconnectedness. Journal of Religion and Health 24:147-153.

Objective: Seeks to identify the defining characteristics of spiritual well-being in older adults. *Sample & Methods*: Uses a qualitative, inductive approach, dependent on patient observation and indepth interviews. Data collected over 18 months from 31 informal, unstructured, and open-ended interviews and 150 hours of participant observation with adults aged 65 to 85 years. Subjects recruited from hospitals, private residences, and high rise elderly units; they were selected on the basis of the investigators' judgements on subjects' spiritual integrity. Categories of individual indicators of spiritual well-being were formed by consensus of the four investigators. *Results*: Spiritual well-being core categories and properties were presented; these were divided into "relationship" (ultimate Other, other/nature, self) and "time" (past, present, future) sections. Spiritual well-being was linked with a present state of peace and harmony, linked to past experiences and future hopes and goals. *Conclusions*: Harmonious interconnectedness (with God, self, and others) was the unifying force between categories and within each identified category. *Quality*: Good.

203. Peterson, E.A. 1985. The physical . . . the spiritual . . . Can you meet all of your patient's needs? Journal of Gerontological Nursing 11(10):23-27.

Objective: Discusses the nurse's task of meeting spiritual needs in older patients. *Sample & Method*: Discussion. *Results & Conclusions*: Must expand the concept of spirituality beyond that of religion, and include among spiritual needs the need for meaning and purpose, forgiveness, love and relationships. The author presents short and long-term spiritual goals for nurses, and provides guidelines on how to best meet those goals. *Quality*: Fair.

204. Brook, V. 1987. The spiritual well-being of the elderly. Geriatric Nursing 8(4):194-195.

Objective: Examines how the spiritual dimension provides meaning to age-related experiences and enhances coping with health problems. *Method*: Review and theoretical integration. *Results & Conclusions*: An elder's spirituality unifies the biological, psychological, and cultural dimensions of life experience. Ericksonian and Piagetian principles of human development may be used to relate life experiences to spirituality. *Quality*: Fair.

205. Sodestrom, K.E., and I.M. Martinson. 1987. Patients' spiritual coping strategies: A study of nurse and patient perspectives. Oncology Nurses Forum 14(2):41-46.
Objective: Describes the spiritual coping strategies of hospitalized patients with cancer and their nurses' awareness of these strategies. *Sample & Methods*: Convenience sample of 25 oncology nurses and 25 of patients (randomly chosen and paired with nurses) from a major nonsectarian medical center in the San Francisco-Oakland area; 68% of patient sample was over age 40 and 64% were White; 76% of nurses under age 30. Nurses and patients were interviewed 30 minutes apart before any verbal interaction could take place. Assessed patients' use of spiritual coping strategies by the Patient Spiritual Coping Interview (PSCI) (McCorkle & Benoliel). Nurses asked to assess the patients' spiritual coping strategies using the same 17 items on the PSCI. *Results*: Spiritual coping strategies used by patients: 84% prayed, 84% asked others to pray *for* them, 64% asked others to pray *with* them, 64% relied on religious objects or music, 64% on religious TV, 56% read Bible, 52% attended church, 36% memorized a Bible verse. 60% of nurses correctly identified patients' use of religious objects or music, 48% identified Bible reading, 40% identified that patients prayed, asked others to pray for and/or with them, and attended church, 28% identified patients' use of religious TV or radio, and 16% identified patients' memorized Bible verse; 56% of nurses could not identify patients' religion. *Conclusions*: Oncology nurses need to recognize the importance of assessing cancer patients' reliance on religious faith and use of spiritual coping. *Quality*: Very good. Enlightening, well-done study.

206. Soeken, K.L., and V.J. Carson. 1987. Responding to the spiritual needs of the chronically ill. Nursing Clinics of North America 22:603-611.
Objective: Discusses the use of a holistic perspective that includes attention to the spirit when caring for the needs of chronically ill patients. *Sample & Methods*: Literature review and discussion. *Results*: Defines and discusses "spirituality" and "spiritual well-being"; examines spiritual aspects of chronic illness and spiritual care during chronic illness; explores how attending to the patient's spirit can help to combat low self-esteem, isolation and loneliness, powerlessness, and anger. *Conclusions*: Nurses can improve the overall care of chronically ill patients by attending to spiritual needs, which may facilitate both emotional and physical healing. *Quality*: Very good;

specifically addresses a nursing audience.

207. Forbis, P.A. 1988. Meeting patients' spiritual needs. Geriatric
      Nursing 9(3):158-159.
Objective: Explores how the nurse can help patients fulfill their spiritual
needs.   Method: Review and theoretical integration.   *Results &
Conclusions*: Spirituality is defined, barriers to integrating spirituality
with nursing care are discussed, and suggestions are made on how
nurses can meet spiritual needs and how they are related to
developmental needs associated with aging. *Quality*: Fair; a practical,
short piece on this vital topic.

208.   DeMarinis, V. 1989.   Spiritual, psychological, and social
       dimensions of pastoral care with patients and families in the
       home health context. Pastoral Psychology 37:275-296.
Objective: Examines the nature, function, and place of pastoral care in
home health care. *Sample & Methods*: Investigator interviewed 37
home health care patients aged 34 to 91 years. *Results*: There is no
single, all-encompassing definition of what the concept of "pastoral
care" means to patients and families in this setting. A variety of
hypotheses concerning the nature and function of pastoral care are
presented. *Conclusions*: There is need for a greater awareness of the
importance of home visitation, expansions of counseling services, and
training of clergy to understand the needs of home-bound elders.
Quality: Fair; an exploratory and hypothesis generating study on a topic
of great importance.

209. Reed, P.G. 1991. Spirituality and mental health in older adults:
      Extant knowledge for nursing. Family and Community Health
      14(2):14-25.
Objective: Examines four sources of knowledge that may enable nurses
to more easily integrate spirituality into the mental health care of older
adults. *Method*: Literature review. *Results*: Sources of knowledge are:
(1) life span theories on development in later life, (2) examples of
spiritual issues that arise during encounters with older patients, (3)
findings from empirical research, and (4) the concept of nurse theorist.
Conclusion: Spirituality may play a significant role in coping with the
aging experience, grief resolution, and in achieving a sense of well-
being and freedom from depression. *Quality*: Good, a theoretical and
integrative paper.

Psychological/Pastoral

210. Holmes, C.B. and M.E. Howard. 1980. Recognition of suicide lethality factors by physicians, mental health professionals, ministers, and college students. Journal of Consulting and Clinical Psychology 48:383-387.

Objective: Examines professionals' ability to recognize persons who are seriously suicidal. *Sample & Methods*: 180 physicians, psychiatrists, psychologists (doctoral level), social workers (masters' level), ministers and lower level college students (30 in each group) were tested for their ability to recognize suicide lethality. All ministers were ordained, seminary trained Christian ministers actively involved in pastoral counseling (6 Catholic priests, 23 Protestant ministers). Each subject completed 13 questions with multiple-choice responses based on the Suicide Potential Rating Scale. The correct responses were summed and the mean for each group of professionals and college students compared. *Results*: Mean scores for each group were as follows: physicians (9.4, SD 1.4), psychiatrists (9.0, SD 1.7), psychologists (7.5, SD 2.4), social workers (6.2, SD 2.4), ministers (5.3, SD 1.8), and college students (5.2, SD 0.8). Differences were significant at p<.01. *Conclusions*: Ministers and low level college students were about equally as likely to recognize the signs of a seriously suicidal patient, and were significantly less likely to do so than other professionals. This study has major implications for the training of ministers in seminary and pastoral counseling programs. *Quality*: Very good. Sobering findings. Highest rates of suicide are among older white men.

211. Reynolds, M.M. 1982. Religious institutions and the prevention of mental illness. Journal of Religion and Health 21(3):245-253.

Objective: Reviews the 1978 recommendations of the President's Commission on Mental Health (PCMH) concerning the involvement of religious institutions in preventing mental health problems. *Sample & Methods*: Report from PCMH (commissioned by President Carter) and discussion of one church program (Cedar Lane Unitarian Church) that developed an extensive adult program that provides emotional support to members of the community. *Results & Conclusions*: Examples of programs that religious institutions can develop to help prevent mental illness are (1) lay caring teams, (2) congregation-based sharing groups (grief, divorce, caregiver support), (3) church-related counseling & growth centers, (4) use of pastoral counselors by community agencies, (5) neighborhood social and civic action, (6) holistic health centers in churches, and (7) publication programs. *Quality*: Good. This article may provide directions for those wishing to develop mental health ministries to the aged in their churches. So much for separation of church and state!

212. Brink, T.L. 1985. The role of religion in later life: A case of consolation and forgiveness. Journal of Psychology and Christianity 4(2):22-25.

Objective: Well-known and respected psychologist examines ways that religion can maintain or restore mental health in later life. *Method*: Case description and discussion. *Results & Conclusions*: Religion may promote mental health in 7 ways: facilitate spiritual fulfillment, enhance socialization, provide forgiveness, help the acceptance of loss, provide practical services, control behavior, and reduce moral outrage. Religion can help elders accept physical disability and an increasing dependence on others. *Quality*: Good.

213. Domino, G. 1985. Clergy's attitudes toward suicide and recognition of suicide lethality. Death Studies 9(3-4):187-199.

Objective: To assess whether clergy can recognize suicidal individuals as well as lay persons or mental health professionals. *Sample & Methods*: 112 clergy members (12 protestants, 25 Catholics, 20 Jewish rabbis, 16 Eastern religious ministers, and 23 nontraditional ministers) were given a "recognition of suicide lethality" scale and a suicide option questionnaire. All clergy were actively involved in pastoral counseling and had been for a minimum of 5 years. *Results*: Clergy were not able to recognize signs of suicidal lethality any better than educated lay-persons, and much less well than mental health professionals. *Conclusions*: The clergy often are involved in counseling with persons who may have high suicidal risk (like the elderly), and therefore need training to recognize suicidal patients and promptly refer them for appropriate care. *Quality*: Good. An eye-opener that stresses the importance of clergy education in this area.

214. Sheinkin, L., and G. Golden. 1985. Therapy with women in the later stages of life: A symbolic quest. Women and Therapy 4 (3):83-92.

Objective: Explores how clinicians can enhance the spiritual growth of elderly women. *Sample & Methods*: Discussion. *Results & Conclusions*: Western culture and religion provide elderly women with few nourishing images that enhance their spirituality and creativity. Recommendations to clinicians are given on how to change this experience through therapy. *Quality*: Fair.

215. Mollica, R.F., F.J. Streets, J. Boascarino, F.C. Redlich. 1986.
      A community study of formal pastoral counseling activities of
      the clergy. American Journal of Psychiatry 143:323-328.
Objective: To comprehensively assess the counseling attitudes and
practices of clergy. *Sample & Methods*: All clergy in south-central
Connecticut (Metropolitan New Haven Directory of Churches and
Synagogues) were sent questionnaires (n = 290), with 74% (214)
completing and returning them (more than half of respondents were 45
years or older). *Results*: The average clergyman spent 2.2 hours per
week counseling. One-third of traditional clergy spent more than 10%
of their time in formal pastoral counseling; Black and evangelical
ministers counseled more than traditional ministers, and the majority
spent 11% to 25% of their time counseling. Marriage, family, and
psychological problems were the most common reason for counseling;
less than 10% of problems were spiritual or religious in nature. Clergy
referred less than 10% of their counselees to specialized mental health
resources. Evangelical clergy made the fewest referrals to mental
health professionals. *Conclusions*: The clergy are important in bridging
the gap between the community and formal mental health services by
helping to get persons into psychiatric treatment. It is likely that clergy
will take an increasingly greater role in the future in referring elderly
persons for needed mental health services. *Quality*: Very good,
although results reflect clergy counseling practices in one specific area
of the country that may not be generalizable.

216. Georgemiller, R.J., and S.H. Getsinger. 1987. Reminiscence
      Therapy: Effects on more and less religious elderly. Journal of
      Religion and Aging 4(2):47-58.
Objective: Investigates the effects of structured group reminiscence on
religious and less religious adults. Sample & Methods: 21 religious and
13 non-religious elders recruited from Chicago area senior centers and
a retirement home. A workshop consisting of 7 weekly 90 minute
reminiscence sessions divided into didactic and experiential sections.
Importance of religion was assessed on a 9-point Likert scale; subjects
were identified as religious if they scored 6-9 and "less religious" for
scores of 5 or less. The Hoge Intrinsic Religious Motivation Scale,
Checklist of Death Attitudes, and Rosenberg Self-Esteem Scale were
also administered. *Results*: Before the intervention, religious persons
were more intrinsically religiously motivated $(p < .001)$ and more
forward-looking toward death $(p < .05)$. After the reminiscence
intervention, the less religious group increased significantly in its level
of meaning in life $(p < .05)$, increased in religiousness from pre- to
posttreatment $(p < .01)$, and demonstrated a reduction in denial of
death $(p < .05)$. No changes were noted for the religious group.

Conclusions: A religious stance may represent a psychological resource for coping with the changes associated with aging; structured reminiscing may foster some of the same positive attitudes in less religious persons. *Quality*: Good.

217.   Larson, D.B., A.A. Hohmann, L.G. Kessler, K.G. Meador, J. Boyd, and E. McSherry. 1988. The couch and the cloth: The need for linkage. Hospital & Community Psychiatry 39:1064-1069.

Objective: To examine and compare types of psychiatric conditions that patients have who see mental health professionals and those who see clergy.   *Sample & Methods*: The 1980-81 NIMH Epidemiologic Catchment Area survey non-randomly sampled community residents in New Haven, Baltimore, St. Louis, Durham, and Los Angeles (n = 26,810) in what was the largest psychiatric epidemiologic study of the decade.   Psychiatric diagnoses and mental health service use were the focus of study; clergy were included as a category of providers. *Results*: Among persons of all ages with mental disorders, 3% saw clergy only, 12% saw mental health specialist only, 3% saw both, and 82% saw neither. Of those who saw clergy only, 10% were over age 65; of those who saw mental health specialists only, 6% were over age 65; of those who saw both, 4% were over age 65; of those who saw neither, 17% were over age 65. Those in the care of clergy only were as likely to have serious mental disorders as those in the care of mental health specialists only. *Conclusions*: Clergy and mental health specialists see patients with mental disorders of similar severity. Clergy are more likely to see older adults with psychiatric problems than are mental health specialists. *Quality*: Very good.

218.   Stuzinski, R. 1988. Transcending a past: From remorse to reconciliation in the aging process. Psychotherapy Patient 5(1-2):207-218.

Objective: This article examines how Judeo-Christian religious beliefs help aging persons overcome regret over past failures and focus on the present and future.   *Sample & Methods*:   Discussion.   *Results & Conclusions*: Remorse or feelings of despair over past failures is an important element in religious growth. Religious rituals and beliefs help to lead the person through a life review process, and eventually a reconciliation of past conflicts. *Quality*: Good.

219.   Bryant, M.D.   1989.   Re-orienting pastoral care with aging persons. Journal of Religion and Aging 5 (3):1-16.

Objective: Argues that changing demographics in the United States will force religious bodies to assume basic responsibility for the spiritual and emotional well-being of elderly persons and their families, requiring a reorientation of pastoral care. *Sample & Methods*: Literature review and discussion. *Results & Conclusions*: Rather than focus on crisis care or individual need, pastoral counseling will need to address the basic problems that older persons face: worsening physical health, increasing dependency, financial insecurity, social isolation and loneliness. Recommendations are made on how the church can reorient pastoral care to address these issues. *Quality*: Good.

220. Lannert, J.L. 1991. Resistance and countertransference issues with spiritual and religious clients. Journal of Humanistic Psychology 31(4):68-76.
Objective: Discusses factors that affect the therapeutic relationship between mental health professionals and religious patients. *Sample & Methods*: Literature review and discussion. *Results & Conclusions*: Secular therapists often have negative biases toward spiritual or religious issues; this is often due to a personal lack of experience with religion, observation of religion's negative expressions of certain patients, lack of knowledge about specific religious doctrines, and personal anxieties over existential issues (such as aging or death) that might be aroused. More valid reasons for displaying caution when dealing with religious issues are ethical concerns such as maintaining personal competence and respect for each client's unique spiritual experiences. *Quality*: Good. This certainly applies to therapy with religious older adults.

221. Waldfogel, S., and P.R. Wolpe. 1993. Using awareness of religious factors to enhance interventions in consultation-liaison psychiatry. Hospital & Community Psychiatry 44:473-477.
Objective: Authors use six dimensions of religious experience to discuss approaches to incorporating religious factors in the psychiatric evaluation and treatment of hospitalized medical patients. *Sample and Methods*: Case series of 6 patients (all under age 50). Results: Ideological, intellectual, ritualistic, experiential, consequential, and supportive dimensions of religion are examined and integrated into the psychiatric care of the medical patient. *Conclusions*: Addressing religious issues can be useful in both the diagnosis and treatment of psychiatric problems in medical patients. *Quality*: Very good. While these authors use younger patients to demonstrate their points, these principles apply equally well, if not more so, to older patients for whom religion is even more likely to play an integral role in their health and well-being.

222. Koenig, H.G. 1993. Trends in geriatric psychiatry of relevance to pastoral counselors. Journal of Religion and Health 32:131-151.
Objective: Examines the increasingly important role of the pastoral counselor in meeting the psychological needs of older adults, provides information on the recognition of common psychiatric syndromes in later life, and reviews the major psychological and biological treatments for these conditions. *Method*: Literature review and discussion. *Results & Conclusions*: As our population ages, government resources shrink, and rates of emotional disorder swell, ministers will be increasingly called upon to recognize, treat, and determine when to refer elders with mental health problems; the importance of educating pastoral staff and church members to perform these tasks is emphasized.

Institutionalized Aged

223. Uhlman, J., and P.D. Steinke. 1984. Pastoral visitation to the institutionalized aged: Delivering more than a lick and a promise. Pastoral Psychology 32:231-238.
Objective: Examines nursing home patients' satisfaction with visits provided by community ministers and facility chaplains. *Sample & Methods*: Nationwide survey of elderly nursing home patients conducted by the Lutheran Council USA; included nursing homes in the urban Midwest, the rural South, the urban East, and the rural West. A total of 120 patients were interviewed; 85% were female, 96% White, 80% over 75 yrs old, 60% from skilled or professional households, 60% institutionalized less than 3 yrs, and 39% non-ambulatory. One-third of participants were Lutherans, one-third Baptists and Methodists, and one-third other denominations. Frequency of visits by clergy and desired frequency were inquired about; length of time spent with patient also examined. *Results*: Only 46% reported receiving regular visits from clergy. Approximately 12% reported a daily or weekly visits from a community pastor (compared with 50% who desired this frequency of visitation); the largest proportion (46%) received monthly visits; and 41% received less than monthly visits (12% wishing this level of visitation). In addition, 39 patients had chaplains available to them; 26% of these received daily or weekly visits from chaplains (compared with 53% of patients who desired such visits); 56% received monthly visits; and 18% received several visits a year or no visits (5% wishing no visits). Time spent with patients on visits was short; 35% of visits by ministers and 76% by chaplains lasted 15 minutes or less; 9% of visits by ministers and 3% of visits by chaplains

lasted more than 45 minutes. *Conclusions*: Visitations by clergy were neither frequent enough or long enough to meet the needs of nursing home patients. Clergy communicated to patients that they had little time to spend with them, causing patients to feel short-changed; this was especially true for elderly patients not receiving visits from family members or friends. Specific needs of patients in this setting were discussed. *Quality*: Very good; a discouraging, but revealing study.

224.   Fisher, G.F. 1990. The role of the chaplain in ministering to persons with Alzheimer's and related disorders. Paper available from chaplain's office, VA Medical Center, Salisbury, NC.
Objective: Provides observations and suggestions on ministering to patients with dementia based on the author's 25 years of experience in a parish setting and 8 years in the VA as a chaplain. *Sample & Methods*: Outline and discussion. *Results & Conclusions*: Provides a list of 11 practical suggestions on how to provide pastoral care to demented elders. Describes how to structure interfaith worship groups for demented elders to enhance spiritual feelings and expression of frustrations. Finally, talks about the chaplain's role as a guide on ethical issues. *Quality*: Excellent. A gold mine of practical hints and suggestions. Nice bibliography.

225.   Richards, M. 1990. Spiritual needs of the cognitively impaired. Generations (Fall issue):63-64.
Objective: Examines the impact of dementia on spirituality and the effects of faith rituals and symbols on elders with dementia. *Sample & Methods*: Theoretical discussion and brief literature review. *Results & Conclusions*: The spiritual needs of the cognitively impaired can be met with religious music, poetry, and symbols that may elicit long-term memories. Both past and current grief issues must also be dealt with. *Quality*: Good. Sensitive discussion.

226.   Richards, M., and S. Seicol. 1991. The challenge of maintaining spiritual connectedness for persons institutionalized with dementia. Journal of Religious Gerontology 7:27-40.
Objective: Explores the types of spiritual interventions that can be useful with demented patients in nursing homes to help maintain quality of life. *Sample & Methods*: Literature review and discussion. *Results:* Authors examine spiritual well-being and discuss how the problem of memory loss can affect it. They discuss the importance of grief and mourning in dementia patients, and the usefulness of spiritual interventions in this regard. The role of caregivers is also examined; the problems that caregivers have in meeting the spiritual needs of the demented is discussed. Finally a method of communicating with

demented patients is described, including an example of a spiritual history and needs assessment form. *Conclusions*: Persons with dementing illnesses have spiritual needs and often respond favorably to religious services and spiritual care. *Quality*: Very Good. Again, very little work has been done on this most important topic. Systematic studies are needed. [Also see Friedman, D. 1995. A life of celebration, meaning, and connection: Facilitating religious life in long-term institutions. In M. Kimble et al (eds.), Aging, Religion, and Spirituality: A Handbook. Minneapolis, MN: Fortress Press.]

Ethical Issues

227. Ley, D.C., and I.B. Corless. 1988. Spirituality and hospice care. Death Studies 12(2):101-110.
Objective: Discusses the importance of addressing spiritual issues in the course of providing hospice care to dying persons. *Sample & Methods*: Discussion. *Results & Conclusions*: Scientific medicine has divided the person into biological and psychological parts, excluding any consideration of the spiritual aspects of human existence. The hospice movement and the aging of the U.S. populations have played an important role in forcing the medical care system's attention to spiritual issues. *Quality*: Good.

228. Koenig, H.G. 1990. Terminal choices: Euthanasia, suicide, and the right to die (by Robert N. Wennberg, 1989, Eerdmans Publishing Co, Grand Rapids, Mich). Journal of the American Geriatrics Society 38:1268-1270.
Objective: Review of a classic book that discusses the issues involved in euthanasia. *Sample & Methods*: Book review. *Results & Conclusions*: Wennberg, a professor of philosophy and a Presbyterian minister, provides a balanced discussion of suicide and euthanasia from a Christian viewpoint. Morally, there is always some "risk" involved when a person takes their own life. This risk, however, depends heavily on the circumstances in which a person finds him or herself. *Quality*: Excellent book. Wennberg treads delicately and artfully the fine moral line involved in this controversial subject.

229. Cohen-Mansfield, J., B.A. Rabinovich, S. Lipson, A. Fein, B. Gerber, S. Weisman, and L.G. Paulson. 1991. The decision to execute a durable power of attorney for health care and preferences regarding the utilization of life-sustaining treatments in nursing home residents. Archives of Internal Medicine 151:289-294.

Objective: Examines nursing home residents' preferences on whom they would choose to make their health care decisions (in the event of incompetence), and assesses preferences for life support in four different <u>hypothetical</u> scenarios of declining cognitive function. *Sample & Methods*: 103 nursing home residents were interviewed and completed questionnaires. *Results & Conclusions*: There was a tendency for patients to choose their children to make health care decisions. The majority of participants did not wish to receive life support in the four scenarios presented to them; nevertheless, there was wide variability in responses. Residents were less likely to want intervention depending on the level of cognitive impairment presented in the scenarios; they were also less likely to want life support if the treatment involved a permanent procedure rather than a temporary one. Religious beliefs were also measured as a variable which affected choices in this regard. *Quality*: Good. Patients' preferences in "hypothetical" scenarios do not always correlate well with their preferences during real life situations.

230.   Cohen-Mansfield, J., J.A. Droge, and N. Billig. 1992. Factors influencing hospital patients' preferences in the utilization of life-sustaining treatments. <u>The Gerontologist</u> 32:89-95.

Objective: Examines older persons preferences for life-sustaining treatments under three <u>hypothetical</u> levels of future cognitive functioning. *Sample & Methods*: Sample consisted of 97 inpatients age 64 yrs or over purposefully selected from Georgetown University Hospital. Patients were surveyed on preferences for treatments (antibiotics, dialysis, permanent respirator support) if they were (1) cognitively intact, (2) confused, or (3) unconscious; sociodemographic characteristics of respondents were assessed, along with current cognitive functioning and depressive symptoms. *Results & Conclusions*: Patients were more likely to want treatment if cognitively intact; 36% did not want treatment in at least 75% of the scenarios presented, whereas 16% wanted treatment in 75% or more of the scenarios. Patients who demonstrated no pattern of preference were more likely to be uneducated and depressed. Preferences were most influenced by personal values, religion, and experiences with illnesses of others. Patients who wanted treatment under all conditions were more religious than others, although the difference only approached significance. *Quality*: Good. Same qualification applies to this study as to their earlier one in nursing home patients.

231.   Koenig, H.G. 1992. Care of the dying. In E. Calkins (ed.), <u>Practice of Geriatrics</u>, 2nd ed. NY: W.B. Saunders co, pp 144-148.

Objective: Examines from a clinical standpoint how to provide high quality care for older patients who are dying. *Sample & Methods*: Literature review and discussion. *Results & Conclusions*: Older persons hold attitudes toward death and dying that are quite different from those of younger persons. These attitudes, and their relationship to religious beliefs and activities, are discussed. Technical advice is given to practitioners on how to deliver high quality "comfort care", both physical and psychological, to help reduce suffering and enhance meaning during the dying process.

232. Koenig, H.G. 1993. Legalizing physician-assisted suicide: Some thoughts and concerns. Journal of Family Practice 37:171-179. Accompanying editorial by Michigan State Medical Society president, Howard Brody.
Objective: Discusses the pros and cons in the debate over whether to legalize physician-assisted suicide (PAS); emphasizes negative consequences. *Sample & Methods*: Review of the literature and discussion. *Results*: Unlike members of the general population, the majority of elderly persons, physicians, lawyers, ethicists and members of the religious community, oppose PAS. Establishing the conditions that warrant PAS (with any degree of certainty) may be difficult if not impossible to achieve in practice, particularly the presence or absence of depression. There is a legitimate concern that PAS may be generalized for use in the non-terminally ill, disabled, elderly, or demented. *Conclusions*: Physicians should determine the underlying reason for the patient's suicidal impulses, and then make every attempt - through medical or psychological means - to alleviate the cause of the suffering. Will stimulate discussion.

233. Siefken, S. 1993. The Hispanic perspective on death and dying: A combination of respect, empathy, and spirituality. Pride Institute Journal of Long Term Home Health Care 12(2):26-28.
Objective: Examines the impact that Hispanic culture has on the needs of dying Hispanic elders. *Sample & Methods*: Discussion. *Results & Conclusions*: A major factors that enhances the dying process for Hispanic elders is having a doctor who is considered one of the family, who focuses on the inner importance of the person, and who has respect for the person's spirituality and religious beliefs. Emphasizes the need to integrate religion into the hospital and home care of elderly Hispanics who are dying. *Quality*: Good.

234. Koenig, H.G. 1994. Hope for the dying. In H. Koenig, Aging and God. NY: Haworth Press, pp 441-461.
Objective: Discusses the issues related to death and dying from both

a Christian and a Jewish viewpoint. *Sample & Methods*: Literature review and discussion. *Results & Conclusions*: Addresses the fear of death that all humans experience and how they deal with it. Provides quotes from the New and Old Testaments of the Bible and from the Talmud about death and the afterlife. Traces Elizabeth Kubler-Ross's change of attitude concerning belief in an afterlife as she progressed through her career. The discussion provides encouragement, hope, meaning, and direction for the dying elder.

235. Shapiro, R.S., A.R. Derse, M. Gottlieb, D. Schiedermayer, and M. Olson. 1994. Willingness to perform euthanasia: A survey of physician attitudes. Archives of Internal Medicine 154:575-584.

Objective: Examines Wisconsin physicians' attitudes toward the practice of euthanasia. *Sample & Methods*: 740 of 2,339 Wisconsin internists, family practitioners, and geriatricians (33%) returned questionnaires about their willingness to perform euthanasia. Physicians' responses were sought to three hypothetical cases of patients requesting euthanasia: 65 yo with mild stroke and depression; 24 yo man with severe painful, disabling injuries from car accident; 65 yo man with late stage Alzheimer's disease, unable to communicate or care for self. *Results*: Seventy percent of physicians were never willing, for any of the cases, to perform euthanasia. Characteristics that differentiated the 30% of physicians who were willing to perform euthanasia from the 70% who were not was specialty (family practice, $p = .04$) and religious affiliation (Jewish or no religion, $p < .001$). *Conclusions*: Religious affiliation is the major factor that distinguishes physicians who would from those who would not perform euthanasia. *Quality*: Very good. This is a concerning finding, given that only a very small fraction of older adults in the United States have similar religious backgrounds to those of physicians most willing to perform euthanasia.

236. Koenig, H.G. 1995. Physicians should not assist in assisted suicide: The case for judicial review. American Journal of Psychiatry, in submission

Objective: Argues that the physician should not be involved in the practice of assisted suicide or euthanasia. *Sample & Methods*: Literature review and discussion. *Results & Conclusions*: The risk of physician involvement in this practice is too high, given personal biases and the difficulty of monitoring. The role of the doctor should remain traditional. If "comfort care" measures and "restriction of food and fluids" are not sufficient to relieve suffering and bring about a good death, then the case should come up for judicial review and the court system should decide based on all available information whether active assistance with dying is indicated. The court would then assign a non-medical technician to carry out the court's decision. A different approach to a complex and controversial subject.

APPLICATIONS IN THE COMMUNITY AND THE CHURCH

237. Steinitz, L.Y. 1981. The local church as support for the elderly. Journal of Gerontological Social Work 4 (2):43-53
Objective: Examines the emergency and on-going services provided by local churches in combating loneliness, providing crisis readjustment, home health care, and practical needs. *Sample & Methods*: Secondary data analysis of data on 81 churches and synagogues in the Chicago area; in-person and telephone interviews with 42 clergymen, 40 lay leaders and elderly congregants, and 38 agency personnel; and indepth participant observation in 15 church-related contexts. Findings are primarily qualitative. *Results*: The most common service provided by churches was the promotion of meaningful contact between congregants and the provision of emotional support to elders suffering from loneliness, malaise, or depression; practical material services was provided on a much less frequent basis and affected only a small number of congregants. Many elderly person, particularly those without families who lived alone, identified the church as their primary source of human contact and emotional support. *Conclusions*: The church often acts as a family surrogate to older persons in the community, is an important source of social contacts, and helps to combat loneliness and isolation among its older members. *Quality*: Fair.

238. Monk, A., and L.W. Kaye. 1982. Gerontological knowledge and attitudes of students of religion. Educational Gerontology 8:435-445.
Objective: Examines the knowledge base that students of religion and graduates have in the area of gerontology. *Sample & Methods*: 142 students of religion and 216 graduates were administered a facts-on-aging quiz and survey that contained questions on myths about aging. *Results & Conclusions*: Low scores on gerontological knowledge and biased attitudes towards the aged were the rule. *Quality*: Good, but disturbing.

239. Cluff, C.B., and L.E. Cluff. 1983. Informal support for disabled persons: A role for religious and community organizations.

Journal of Chronic Disease 12:815-820.
Objective: Examines the role of religious communities in providing support to chronically ill and dependent persons; audience is physicians and other health care providers. *Method*: Literature review and discussion. *Results and Conclusions*: Religious organizations have traditionally supported the ill and infirm, and are well-suited both in philosophy and in man-power to do so. The few attempts by religious congregations to meet the needs of sick elders have often lacked outreach into the community and linkage with formal agencies and professional health care providers. Churches need to develop better organized informal volunteer support programs for needy elders. *Quality*: Fair; calls for a vital need.

240. Moberg, D.O. 1983. Compartmentalization and parochialism in religious and voluntary action research. Review of Religious Research 24:318-321
Objective: Examines and critiques the way religious activity has been operationalized in voluntary action research. *Sample & Methods*: Literature review and discussion. *Results & Conclusions*: Membership and activity in primary religious bodies is often excluded from research examining voluntary activities of adults. This is unfortunate given that church members are more likely than non-members to be involved in voluntary community activities; furthermore, participation in church and synagogues often continues long after aging forces them to drop out of other community organizations. *Quality*: Very good.

241. Moberg, D.O. 1983. The ecological fallacy: Concerns for program planners. Generations 8 (1):12-14.
Objective: Provides a state of the art review of the attitudes of gerontologists toward religion, the importance of religion to the elderly, and religion's relevance to aging organizations. *Sample & Methods*: Literature review and discussion. *Results & Conclusions*: Cooperation between aging organizations and religious groups is essential, since the latter can become one of the most significant supporters of gerontological services. *Quality*: Excellent. By a true giant in the field.

242. Hateley, B.J. 1984. Spiritual well-being through life histories. Journal of Religion and Aging 1(2):63-71.
Objective: Describes an educational program for use in churches that can increase personal insight and spiritual well-being among older congregants. *Method*: Program described and comments of participants reviewed. *Results & Conclusions*: This program utilizes lectures, writing assignments, and group discussions to help elders through transition periods by exploring their faith experience as it has

unfolded throughout their lives (autobiographical approach). *Quality*: Good; program has been implemented in various settings with encouraging results.

243. Haver, D. 1984. Church-based programs for Black care-givers of non-institutionalized elders. Journal of Gerontological Social Work 5:43-55.

Objective: Examines the operation and impact of a church-based program to train and provide mutual support to family caregivers of older Black adults. *Sample & Methods*: 282 caregivers from the Washington, DC, area participated in programs at eight church sites; a 12 hour caregiving program was administered at each of the sites and outcomes before and after measured using the OARS scale. *Results & Conclusions*: Mutual help groups were successful with initiating multiple projects, involving hundreds of church members; cooperation between different churches operating at a single community site produced the most successful mutual self-help groups; the training program, unfortunately, was not successful with fostering new caregiving activities or with forming linkages with formal service providers. *Quality*: Good. These caregivers were experiencing very little caregiver burden; it might be interesting to examine the effects of a similar program initiated among White caregivers, who have a less well developed system of social supports than do Blacks.

244. Johnson, P.T. and M.J. Van Meter. 1984. Family decision making, long-term care for the elderly, and the role of religious organizations: I. The issues and the challenge. Journal of Religion and Aging 1(3):61-69.

Objective: Explores the role of the church in providing education and support for the family caregivers of chronically ill older adults. *Sample & Methods*: Literature review and discussion. *Results & Conclusions*: Families are largely responsible for providing social support, psychological support, and direct physical care for frail elders with physical illness. Given that persons age 85 or over are the fastest growing age group in the United States and that women are increasingly joining the work force (decreasing their availability to provide care at home), there is an increasing need for education and support of families with aging members. The church provides a natural setting where support groups for adult child caregivers can form and receive education about their own aging, perceptions their children may have about aging, balancing roles at home and work, and future decision regarding long-term care concerning their aging parents. *Quality*: Good.

245. Westberg, G.F. 1984. Churches are joining the health care
     team. Urban Health, October issue:34-36
Objective: Discusses the role that churches can play in screening for
medical and psychiatric illness, and how this might be practically
accomplished. *Sample & Methods*: Dr. Westberg discusses 12
healthful activities typically engaged in by churches, his own
development of Holistic Health Centers, and the Parish Nurse Project.
Results & Conclusions: Churches are perfectly positioned to work with
the medical and social service agencies to enhance the health and well-
being of citizens of all ages. *Quality*: Fair.

246. Wylie, W.E. 1984. Health counseling competencies needed by
     the minister. Journal of Religion and Health 23(3):237-249.
Objective: Examines the health counseling typically given by Church of
Christ ministers, and explores areas of needed training that should be
obtained during seminary or continuing education classes. *Sample &
Methods*: Questionnaires were completed by 108 ministers in five
states. *Results & Conclusions*: These pastors typically counseled
persons concerning marital problems, individual issues, alcohol or drug
abuse problems, death education, and aging-related topics. The
majority of ministers indicated they had not received adequate training
for such health counseling. Recommendations are made on how to
correct this deficiency in seminary training. *Quality*: Good.

247. Barden, A.K. 1985. Toward new directions for ministry in aging:
     An overview of issues and concepts. Journal of Religion and
     Aging 2(1-2):137-150.
Objective: Discusses the leadership role of the church in the field of
aging. *Method*: Theoretical discussion. *Results & Conclusions*:
Themes of religiosity, religion, theology, spirituality, and ministry are
discussed. Suggests that the developmental and holistic goal of the
church's involvement in aging is spiritual well-being. *Quality*: Fair;
addresses an important topic, given the need for a more active role by
the church in providing both spiritual and psychological support for
aging members.

248. Becker, A.H. 1985. Pastoral theological implications of the aging
     process. Journal of Religion and Aging 2(3):13-30.
Objective: Discusses the spiritual and theological issues related to three
epochs of aging (young-old, middle-old, and old-old). *Method*:
Theoretical discussion. *Results & Conclusions*: Young-old are
concerned with what the individual should do with his/her life; middle-
old struggle with issues related to dying; old-old must deal with
suffering. The process of life-review is recommended when working

with older adults, and other ways are suggested by which the clergy can respond to the needs of older adults. *Quality*: Fair.

249. Bronte, D.L. 1985. The third quarter of life: Implications for American religious institutions. Journal of Religion and Aging 2(1-2):117-125.
Objective: Explores the implications of an aging society, extended periods of time in retirement, and unused energy and talent of persons in the latter third of their lives (ages 50 to 75). *Sample & Methods*: Discussion. *Results & Conclusions*: The majority of congregants in mainline Protestant churches are currently in the third quarter of life; this has implications for religious institutions who are called to help persons utilize their talents and nurture individual spiritual and emotional growth.

250. Ellor, J.W., and R.B. Coates. 1985. Examining role of the church in the aging network. Journal of Religion and Aging 2(1-2):99-116.
Objective: Examines services and programs for the elderly found in local churches. *Sample & Methods*: Interviews with clergy, social service personnel, and elderly persons were conducted in six communities over a four year period. *Results & Conclusions*: The findings of this survey are discussed in light of (1) the role of the church in providing for the social, psychological, and spiritual needs of older adults, (2) how local churches can be linked up both with each other and with social service agencies to help serve the elderly, and (3) how to provide knowledge about aging issues to the clergy. *Quality*: Good. A prophetic article that both social service agencies and clergy will look to as social and psychological problems of older adults become more real and insoluble in the future - demanding such cooperation.

251. Hendrickson, M.C. 1985. The role of the church in aging: Implications for policy and action. Journal of Religion and Aging 2(1-2):5-16.
Objective: Explores the roles and responsibilities of churches in meeting the social and psychological needs of older adults. *Sample & Methods*: Discussion. *Results & Conclusions*: Church bodies from a wide range of denominations and traditions should unite together to form a coalition dedicated to helping serve the needs of elderly persons in their congregations. More research in the area and education of church leaders is necessary for this to come about. *Quality*: Good. See Ellor and Coates below.

252. Morris, J.N. 1985. Issues in publicly subsidized long term care systems and implications for the religious sector (1984 National Symposium on the Church and Aging, Zion, Illinois). Journal of Religion and Aging 2(1-2):151-163.
Objective: Examines the social responsibility of the church in meeting the needs of elders requiring long-term care. *Sample & Methods*: Review and discussion. *Results*: Among other responsibilities, the church needs to increasingly act as an advocate to influence public policy, provide practical services and housing, and serve as an education resource for advice and referral. *Conclusions*: The church must assist in "bridging the gap" that is resulting from an explosion of chronically ill elders and dwindling federal and state support for this group. *Quality*: Good. Note that this article predates the Koenig, George, and Schneider (1994) paper by 10 years; unfortunately, the church has yet to fully implement its leadership role in this regard (nor has the government provided any incentives for churches to do so).

253. Rowles, G.D. 1985. The rural elderly and the church. Journal of Religion and Aging 2(1-2):79-98.
Objective: Examines the role of the church in the lives of the rural elderly, including how the former can help meet the unique aging challenges that the latter face. *Sample & Methods*: A 7 year ethnographic study of 15 rural elders aged 62-91 years. *Results & Conclusions*: The church plays a central role in the lives of rural elderly. The author suggests that the church needs to (1) increase its accessibility to this group, (2) complement (not duplicate) secular service programs, (3) facilitate the development of support networks, and (4) provide health education. *Quality*: Fair.

254. Sheinkin, L., and G. Golden. 1985. Therapy with women in the later stages of life: A symbolic quest. Women and Therapy 4(3):83-92.
Objective: Examines women's spiritual and psychological issues in later life. *Method*: Theoretical discussion. *Results & Conclusions*: There are unique difficulties that older women face in their spiritual evolution, given that Western culture and institutionalized religion offer few nourishing images for aging women. Clinicians can help elderly women to change this experience and meet their potential. *Quality*: Fair; one of the few commentaries that focuses specifically on women's issues. Note, however, that despite having few role models, elderly women are the most religious element in our society.

255. Sherwood, S., and E. Bernstein. 1985. Informal care for vulnerable elderly: Suggestions for church involvement.

Journal of Religion and Aging 2(1-2):55-67.
Objective: Discusses the role of the church as a provider of informal support for older adults. *Sample & Methods*: Review and discussion. *Results & Conclusions*: Church can help in a number of ways, such as acting as an advocate, organizing volunteer services, setting up blood banks, and providing many other practical services. *Quality*: Good; basic idea is similar to Shepherds' Center approach.

256. Koenig, H.G. 1986. Shepherds' Centers: Elderly people helping themselves. Journal of the American Geriatrics Society 34:73
Objective: Comments on a rapidly growing community program to meet the needs of the frail elderly, which is operated and run by older adults themselves. *Method*: Program review and commentary. *Results & Conclusions*: This effort represents a grass-roots interdenominational effort (depending entirely on private funds) to mobilize the unused talents of healthy elders to meet the needs of their sick, disabled peers; holds great promise at a time when federal and state funds for aging programs are limited or being cut back. Over the past 10 years, Shepherd's Centers have sprung up rapidly throughout America, with over 1800 congregations affiliated with 90 centers nationwide in 1994.

257. Netting, F.E., and C.C. Wilson. 1986. Educating professionals to understand religious sponsorship of long term care facilities. Gerontology and Geriatrics Education 7(1):25-34.
Objective: Examines what it means for a nursing home or retirement community to be "affiliated" with a religious organization. *Sample & Methods*: Literature review, presentation of a teaching model and discussion. *Results*: Provides a teaching model whose objective is to (1) sensitize professionals in aging to complex issues surrounding sponsorship of long term care facilities by religious bodies, (2) discuss major issues involved in religious sponsorship, and (3) provide strategies for dealing with legal, financial, and other problems in this area. *Conclusions*: Aging professionals need to be educated about the meaning of religious sponsorship of LTC facilities, and the problems that may arise. *Quality*: Very good; a neglected topic that deserves focused attention, given the future likelihood of an increased role for religious institutions in providing care for elders in our society.

258. Payne, B.P. 1986. Sex and the elderly: No laughing matter in religion. Journal of Religion and Aging 3 (fall-winter):141-152.
Objective: Examines the prevalent myths about aging that sex is for the young and religion is for the old. *Sample & Methods*: Literature review and discussion. *Results & Conclusions*: A number of demographic and social changes in church membership are likely to deeply affect

congregations in the areas of sex and religion: (1) transition from younger congregations to largely adult membership, (2) transition from mostly male members to mostly female members, (3) transition from predominantly married to many single members (due to death of spouse or divorce), (4) increasing numbers of persons with multiple choice lifestyles, and (5) changes in attitudes from exclusive to inclusive. Implications for religious bodies are discussed. *Quality*: Very good; however, these findings apply largely to liberal and mainline Protestant traditions.

259. Tobin, S.S., J. Ellor, and S.M. Anderson-Ray. 1986. Enabling the Elderly: Religious Institutions Within the Community Service System. Albany: State University of New York Press.
Objective: Examines the role that religious institutions can play within the community social service system. *Sample & Methods*: Literature review and discussion. *Results & Conclusions*: Provides a state of the art review and discussion of contributions of the church and ways these contributions can be integrated with current government-sponsored services for the elderly. *Quality*: Very good.

260. Adams, R.G, and B.J. Stark. 1987. Church conservatism and services for the elderly. Journal of Religion and Aging 4(3-4): 69-85.
Objective: Examines the relationship between churches' provision of services for the elderly, linkages with local aging social service network, and social conservatism. *Sample & Methods*: Mail survey of 79 church pastors in a rural North Carolina county. Data were analyzed by linear regression and factor analysis. *Results*: Conservative churches provided fewer services to the elderly than did liberal churches; degree of fundamentalism did not predict failure to provide services. *Conclusions*: Conservative churches tend to provide fewer services for aging adults and collaborate less often with aging social service agencies. *Quality*: Fair. One of the reasons for this may be that a much greater proportion of the congregants of liberal and mainline traditions are over age 65 than are those from conservative denominations, thereby providing more initiative for such linkages.

261. Koenig, H.G. 1987. Shepherds' Centers: Role of the physician. Geriatric Consultant 5(4):6-7.
Objective: Examines the role that the physician can play in helping to support and, as a retired physician, becoming actively involved in Shepherds' Centers. *Sample & Methods*: Discussion. *Results & Conclusions*: There are many ways in which retired physicians can become involved in Shepherds' Centers, including teaching classes on

health topics, providing brief screening exams, as well as offering their expertise on administrative matters. These health professionals have spent their lives easing the suffering of others, and being able to continue in this role (now in a voluntary manner) can be immensely rewarding.

262. Netting, F.E. 1987. Religiously affiliated continuum of care retirement communities. Journal of Religion and Aging 4(1):51-66.
Objective: In 1929, 80% of homes of the aged were operated by religious or private organizations; today 59% are so sponsored. This study examines the meaning of religious sponsorship for nine religiously affiliated continuum of care retirement communities (CCRCs). *Sample & Methods*: A semi-structured interview schedule was administered to representatives of nine CCRC's in Arizona. To be selected, the CCRC had to have at least three levels of housing or health care, had to be a non-profit corporation, and had to have a publicly acknowledged relationship with a religious group or groups. *Results*: Meaning of religious sponsorship, including the advantages, disadvantages, and influence on quality of care, was examined. Seven models or types of CCRC's were described, from a "religious order model" to a "corporate intermediary model." *Conclusions*: Religious sponsorship of nursing homes and retirement communities is very common, but the nature of sponsorship is changing in today's financial and medical-legal climate. *Quality*: Good.

263. Rogal, S.J. 1987. John Wesley's eighty-seventh year: Good is the work of the Lord. Journal of Religion and Aging 4(1):67-77.
Objective: Examines John Wesley's last 14 months of life and his accomplishments during that time. *Sample and Methods*: Historical review and discussion. *Results & Conclusions*: Despite major physical illness, Wesley spent the last year of his life as an evangelical missionary traveling and preaching throughout Great Britain, as well as administering the details of the Methodist organization. "Wesley did not seek to avoid old age; he simply never considered it!" *Quality*: Very good. Provides a different type of role model for those who think fatigue, social withdrawal, and disengagement are normal for persons in late life.

264. Sapp, S. 1987. An alternative Christian view of aging. Journal of Religion and Aging 4(1):1-13.
Objective: To elaborate a Christian view of aging that is realistic and takes into account the very real losses involved. *Sample & Methods*:

Literature review and theoretical discussion. *Results & Conclusions*: Most Christian writing about the aged has been affirmative, picturing late life as a time of fulfillment and maturity to be "eagerly awaited and embraced." This not the case for many, many older adults. Focusing on a theology of the Cross, Sapp emphasizes that loss and suffering are a part of human existence. This view helps the older person to realize that they need God and are not entirely self-sufficient. This view of aging emphasizes the value of the person, rather than of their productivity. *Quality*: Excellent theoretical piece that discards the rose-colored glasses of contemporary thought to take a real look at the aging process and its implications.

265. Stafford, T. 1987. The graying of the church. <u>Christianity Today</u>, November 6:17-22.
Objective: Examines impact of changing age-composition of U.S. church congregations, where the proportion of members age 65 or older is becoming larger and larger (mainline Protestant denominations, in particular). Also discusses whether older church leaders should eagerly step aside to make room for younger leaders, and what roles older church members might play. *Sample and Methods*: Review of popular literature and discussion. *Results & Conclusions*: One-quarter of Presbyterians, Episcopalians, and Methodists are age 65 or over, and 50% are over age 50. When the baby boomers reach age 65, payroll taxes for social security may increase from the current level of 8 percent to 25 or 30 percent to maintain current benefits, perhaps creating a war between generations. Previous images of America will be hard to uphold when this nation becomes a nation of retirees. The response of the church to this brewing crisis is discussed. "Leisure" and "loss" are the two needs that will have to be met. Churches need ministries not only to the home-bound and nursing home, but also to its healthy elders. Emphasizes that the money, time, and energy of older persons is more available for church service than it is that of younger persons, who may have energy, but seldom devote it to the church. *Quality*: Excellent contemporary discussion of the major challenges that churches will increasingly face in this area, emphasizing the unique talents of the elderly and how they can be used to meet the needs of frail elders in their congregations.

266. Olson, L.M., J. Reis, L. Murphy, and J.H. Gehm. 1988. The religious community as a partner in health care. <u>Journal of Community Health</u> 13 (4):249-257.
Objective: Examines the possible role that Black inner-city churches might play in sponsoring new maternal and child health programs. *Sample & Methods*: Indepth interviews were conducted with

representatives from 176 inner-city churches (mostly Baptist, south-side of Chicago) concerning perceptions of social and health problems of women and children, and the role that the church might take in helping to solve these problems. *Results & Conclusions*: Only a small number of churches had ongoing programs for youths or mothers. While there was interest in expanding services, few churches had the necessary staff, funds, or technical expertise to conduct such programs. *Quality*: Good. While this report does not concern older adults, it provides information about the barriers that churches are likely to face in developing new programs for any needy group (including the elderly).

267. Sheehan, N.W., R. Wilson, and L.M. Marella. 1988. The role of the church in providing services for the aging. Journal of Applied Gerontology 7:231-241.

Objective: Examines the prevalence of church-based aging programs, factors related to their development, and linkages between churches and social agencies. *Sample & Methods*: The state of Connecticut was divided into 5 regions with 200 churches and synagogues selected from each region using a stratified sample to ensure 40% Catholic, 40% Protestant, and 20% Jewish. Completed surveys were received from 212 of these religious bodies (21% response rate); sample breakdown consisted of 25% Catholic churches, 71% Protestant churches, and 5% Jewish synagogues. Congregation sizes averaged 100 to 500 members. The mean proportion of elderly members in these congregations was 26%. *Results*: Churches reported between 0 and 11 service programs for aging congregants (mean, 4 programs). Most common were visitation programs for the homebound (84%), for nursing home residents (80%), and for hospitalized elders (70%). Other programs included transportation services (44%), telephone reassurance (37%), social/recreational activities (32%), food distribution (26%), education/discussion groups (26%), home-delivered meals (16%), support groups for caregivers (14%), and self-help groups for seniors (7%). Size of congregation, percentage of older members, and religion did not predict total number of church-based programs. Clergy indicated the following areas as their first priority: providing information about services (26%), information on aging (10%), information on health and illness (9%), family dynamics (9%), and religious programs for older adults (6%). Only one-third of clergy (35%) admitted to being interested in attending educational programs on aging related issues. *Conclusions*: Besides visitation programs, the range of services offered to older adults was distinctly limited. While 72% of churches identified the elderly a priority group over the next 5-10 years, only one-third of clergy had enough interest to want to attend educational programs on aging issues. *Quality*: Very good. A sad commentary on churches' interest in their older congregants. Given a response rate of only 21%, it is likely that these churches were probably biased towards having more programs for the aged - making this is a best case scenario.

268. Wilson, V., and F.E. Netting. 1988. Exploring the interface of local churches with the aging network: A comparison of Anglo and Black congregations. Journal of Religion and Aging 5(1-2):51-60.

Objective: Examines ministers' attitudes toward working with social service agencies to provide services to older adults. *Sample & Method*: Survey of 19 ministers from White churches and 8 ministers from Black churches. *Results*: Black ministers strongly agreed that churches should merge their local programs with social service agencies to enhance service delivery to older adults; White ministers were more mixed in their agreement. Black and White ministers were unclear on whether elders sought help first from their local church or from social service agencies. Black ministers perceived a gap between churches and social service agencies, while Anglo ministers were less likely to do so. Both Black and Anglo ministers agreed that churches should work closely with social service agencies in the community, and that the meeting of spiritual versus material needs should not be separated and met only by agencies that specialize in these areas. *Conclusion*: The church is a potential resource for bridging the gap between services offered by government-sponsored social agencies and the efficient and timely delivery of those services to older adults. *Quality*: Fair.

269. Brewer, E.D. 1989. A national study of gerontology in theological education. Journal of Religion and Aging 6(1-2):15-29.

Objective: Examines the amount of gerontological education that theological schools provide for seminarians. *Sample & Methods*: Questionnaires completed by 113 seminaries of 20 different denominations in the United States. *Results & Conclusions*: There was evidence for increasing gerontological education in seminaries, although still less than adequate. The paper provides a guide for increasing education in this area, including a list of courses on aging, teaching methods, and qualifications of faculty. *Quality*: Very good.

270. Dickerson, B.E., D.R. Myers, and L.E. Coleman. 1989. Southwestern Baptist Theological Seminary and Baylor University: Ministerial gerontological education. Journal of

Religion and Aging 6 (1-2):103-122.
Objective: Provides an example of a cooperative effort between a theological seminary and a private university to enhance gerontological education of ministers. *Sample & Methods*: Description of program. *Results & Conclusions*: Paper describes (1) the joint efforts of both programs to provide seminarians with a gerontological education, (2) the factors necessary for successful cooperation between a seminary and a university, and (3) problems encountered and needing to be resolved to continue such a joint effort. *Quality*: Fair.

271. Moberg, D.O. 1990. Religion and aging. In K.F. Ferraro (ed), Gerontology: Perspectives and Issues. New York: Springer, pp 179-205.
Objective: Provides an overview on religion and aging, interpreting research findings and discussing implications for churches and for public policy. *Sample & Methods*: Literature review and discussion. *Results & Conclusions*: Religion plays many important roles, both social and psychological, in the lives of older adults. Churches provide a range of social and practical services to elderly members. Nevertheless, older adults still face problems in organized religion; these problems need to be better understood.

272. Payne, B.P. 1990. Research and theoretical approaches to spirituality and aging. Generations 14(4):11-14.
Objective: Explores theories about aging and spirituality, and reviews definitions of religion, religiosity, and spirituality. *Sample & Methods*: Literature review and discussion. *Results & Conclusions*: Concept of cohort and period effects provides a framework by which to understand changes in spirituality with aging and to expand sources of spirituality beyond the traditional. *Quality*: Very Good. See also : Payne, B.P. 1982. Religiosity. In D. Mangen, W. Peterson (eds), Social Roles and Social Participation. Minneapolis: University of Minnesota Press; and Payne, B.P. 1985. Religious life of the elderly: Myth or reality? In C. Lefevre, P. Lefevre (eds), Aging and the Human Spirit. Chicago: Exploration Press.

273. Custer, C.C. 1991. The church's ministry and the coming of the aged. Circuit Rider (September issue) (Nashville, TN: Methodist Publishing House).
Objective: Examine issues related to aging member of the Methodist church. *Method*: Discussion. *Results & Conclusions*: By the year 2000, nearly 50% of all Methodists in the United States will be over the age of 60. These demographic figures have enormous implications for the agenda of the Methodist church in the coming decades.

Quality: Good. An eye-opener.

274. Lewis, A.M. 1991. The middle aging of America: Spiritual and
educational dilemmas for clergy education. Journal of Religious
Gerontology 7(4):47-53.
Objective: Examines the effect of an increasingly large population of
middle-aged Americans on the preparedness of clergy to meet the
needs of this population, focusing on the lack of training the seminaries
typically provide students on aging and gerontological issues. *Sample
& Methods*: Discussion. *Results & Conclusions*: Adult development
and gerontology needs to be incorporated into the curriculum of
seminary programs to help future clergy meet the needs of this
increasingly large component of their churches. Suggestions for
incorporation are included. *Quality*: Good.

275. Pieper, H.G., and T. Garrison. 1992. Knowledge of social
aspects of aging among pastors. Journal of Religious
Gerontology 8(4):89-105.
Objective: Surveyed pastors on how much they knew about the key
social aspects of aging. *Sample & Methods*: A random sample of 400
pastors located in Indiana were mailed a questionnaire with the aging
questions; 160 questionnaires were returned (40%). The average
pastor was age 47, had been in the ministry for at least 20 years, and
had a congregation with an average of 223 members. *Results*: Out of
a possible 100, the average pastor scored only 55%. Seventeen of the
20 questions (85%) were answered incorrectly by at least one-third of
the ministers. Note that only 30% of pastors reported covering
gerontology related topics during seminary. Less than one-fourth of
the pastors' congregations had assistance program to provide concrete
help for elderly members of the congregation - despite the fact that
over 50% of these congregations had one-third or more of their
membership aged 65 or older. Knowledge about aging was positively
correlated with such programs. *Conclusions*: Pastors' level of general
knowledge about aging was surprisingly low, despite large numbers of
elderly persons in their congregations. Pastors' knowledge about aging
predicted whether their churches would have special programs to meet
the needs of elderly congregants. *Quality*: Very good. A sad
commentary on pastors' knowledge about aging; if anything, these
figures are probably an overestimate, given that pastors with little
interest in or knowledge about aging probably didn't return the
questionnaire (i.e., were disproportionately represented among the
60% of nonresponders).

276.   Koenig, H.G., L.K. George, and R. Schneider. 1994.   Mental
       health care for older adults in the year 2020: A dangerous and
       avoided topic. The Gerontologist 34:674-679.
Objective: Alerts gerontologists and health care policy makers to the
impact that Medicare reimbursement policies is having on older adults'
access to mental health care and the future effect it will have when the
center of the 80 million baby boom cohort reaches age 65. *Methods*:
Literature review and discussion. *Results & Conclusions*: A combined
effort by secular and religious organizations will be needed to avert the
mental health care crisis ahead; churches (working together through
community programs like Shepherd's Centers) have an opportunity to
take a leading role in this regard.

277.   Thomas, L.E., and S.A. Eisenhandler (eds.). 1994. Aging and
       the Religious Dimension. Westport, CT: Auburn House.
Objective: Examines how aging affects religion and vice versa. *Sample
& Methods*: An edited book *Results & Conclusions*: This book consists
of 13 chapters focusing on the religious dimension in aging. Includes
a chapter on how the older person's sense of spirituality functions to
promote concern for others (Rubenstein). *Quality*: Good.

RESEARCH ON AGING CLERGY

278.   Margraff, R.L. 1986. Aging: Religious sisters facing the future.
       Women and Politics 6(2):35-49.
Objective: Examines the changing demographics of women religious
and the effects that this will have on the future of this religious order.
Sample & Methods: Observations on 840 elderly sisters from 3
congregations comprise the data for this report.   *Results &
Conclusions*: The entry of young women into religious orders has
decreased and the average age of sisters is well above that of the
general population. Problems that aging sisters are likely to encounter
include retirement from an active work life, housing, medical care,
economic concerns, and others. These concerns for the future are
addressed in the paper. *Quality*: Good.

279.   Schoenherr, R.C., L.A. Young, and J.P. Vilarino.   1988.
       Demographic transitions in religious organizations: A
       comparative study of priest decline in Roman Catholic dioceses.
       Journal for the Scientific Study of Religion 27:499-523.
Objective: Examines the effects that demographic changes in the
distribution of priests in the Catholic Church may have on structural

change within the church. *Sample & Methods*: Data on the changing size and distribution of Catholic priests were obtained from a 19 year census-registry for two dioceses (a U.S. and a Spanish). Results: Between 1966 and 1984, these dioceses lost 15% (U.S.) and 30% (Spanish) of their practicing priests; projected losses by the year 2000 were at 50% or more. The entire population of Catholic clergy are aging rapidly and a relatively large new group of young priests are moving up through the ranks. Implications for doctrinal changes within the church are discussed. Also see Young et al 1992 (ref # 282).

280.   Chen, M.Y.T, and J.L. Goodwin. 1991. The continuity perspective of aging and retirement applied to Protestant clergy: An analysis of theory. Journal of Religious Gerontology 7 (3):55-67.

Objective: Examines theories of aging and retirement as they might apply to Protestant clergy. *Sample & Methods*: Literature review and discussion. *Results & Conclusions*: The continuity theory best describes the pattern of retirement seen in Protestant clergy. *Quality*: Good. Has 44 references.

281.   Goodwin, J.L, and M.Y.T. Chen. 1991. From pastor to pensioner: A study of retired Canadian Protestant clergy from the continuity perspective. Journal of Religious Gerontology 7 (3):69-79.

Objective: Examines the adjustment to retirement of Protestant clergy using a continuity model. *Sample & Methods*: A convenience sample of 185 Anglican, Baptist, and United Church of Christ retired clergy in Canada (Atlantic side) were mailed questionnaires and then interviewed to gather data on adjustment to retirement. *Results & Conclusions*: The four major findings generally supported a continuity theory: (1) clergy tended to maintain their lifestyles prior to retirement, (2) retired clergy continue with existing activities, rather than taking up new ones, (3) retirement is facilitated by the occupational subculture of these religious groups, (4) responses of clergy to stress and crisis remain unchanged after retirement. *Quality*: Very good. An increasingly important topic on which there is very little data.

282.   Young, L.A., R.A. Schoenherr, and D.R. Hoge. 1992. The changing age distribution and theological attitudes of Catholic priests revisited. Sociological Analysis 53 (1):73-87.

Objective: Provides new data to confirm earlier reports of large numbers of older priests and, consequently, a shift toward conservative religious orientation in the priesthood. *Sample & Methods*: Data gathered from 86 dioceses. *Results & Conclusions*: Due to both aging and cohort effects, increasing numbers of older priests coupled with a shift toward conservatism among younger priests, an increasingly conservative Catholic clergy is expected.   *Quality*: Very good. Providing for the increasingly large number of elderly priests has caused a near monetary crisis for the Catholic church. Also see Shoenherr et al 1988 (ref 279).

Part IV

Measuring Religiosity and Spirituality

MEASURING RELIGIOSITY AND SPIRITUALITY

283. Paloutzian, R.F., and C.W. Ellison. 1982. Loneliness, spiritual well-being, and the quality of life. In A. Peplau, D. Perlman (eds.), Loneliness: A Sourcebook of Current Theory, Research, and Therapy. NY: Wiley InterScience, pp 224-237.

Objective: Authors develop a spiritual well-being (SWB) scale that measures both general life satisfaction (existential well-being) and religious well-being. *Sample & Methods*: Generated 10 existential items (without reference to God) and 10 religious well-being items (with reference to God); half of all items were worded positively and half negatively to avoid response bias. Scale was then administered to 206 students from three religious colleges, and factor analysis was used to demonstrate that items clustered together. *Results*: The scale yields three scores (1) total SWB score, (2) religious well-being score, and (3) existential well-being score. Test-retest reliability coefficients and alpha coefficients of internal consistency were high. *Conclusions*: This SWB scale can be used as an overall quality of life measure, a measure of life-satisfaction / life-direction, or a measure of religious well-being. *Quality*: Good. Experience with use in older adults is developing. Must remember that this SWB scale measures both existential and religious well-being; therefore, only the religious well-being subscale should be used when attempting to measure associations between psychological health and spirituality.

284. Florian, V., and S. Kravetz. 1983. Fear of personal death: Attribution, structure, and relation to religious belief. Journal of Personality and Social Psychology 44(3):600-607.

Objective: Investigates whether individuals attribute the fear of their own death to intrapersonal, interpersonal, or transpersonal consequences of mortality. *Sample & Methods*: 178 adult male Jews aged 18 to 30 (mean 22 years); composed of university students, orthodox Jewish religious school students, and military cadets in Israel. A Fear of Personal Death scale was used, along with the Jewish Religiosity Index. *Results & Conclusions*: The religious group attributed more fear of punishment in the hereafter and less fear of self-annihilation. One aspect of being an observant Jew is believing in immortal accountability. *Quality*: Fair. The only reason for including this study is because a Jewish Religiosity Index was utilized to measure religiousness (Ben-Meir, Y., and P. Kedem. 1979. Index of religiosity of the Jewish population of Israel. Megamot 24:353-362). This is the only index of its kind that I am aware of. I had it translated from Hebrew into English by Rabbi Dayle A. Friedman, chaplain at the Philadelphia Geriatric Center. For a copy, contact me at Box 3400, Duke University Medical Center, Durham, NC 27710.

285. Moberg, D.O. 1984. Subjective measures of spiritual well-being. Review of Religious Research 25(4):351-364.
Objective: Describes the development an instrument to measure spiritual well-being (SWB). *Sample and Method*: The 10-subscale instrument was developed in the following manner. Factor analysis of items from survey research in Sweden and the United States resulted in seven subscales that relate to the Christian faith, self-satisfaction, and personal piety; three more subscales were added to measure involvement in political, religious, and charitable volunteer service activities. *Results & Conclusions*: The instrument or its subscales can be used for scientific, clinical and evaluative purposes. *Quality*: Good; note again however, that inclusion of indexes dealing with life-satisfaction are included within the instrument and may confound the relationship between SWB and psychological health in studies that examine this association.

286. Moberg, D.O. 1985. Spirituality and science: The progress, problems, and promise of scientific research on spiritual well-being. Paper presented at Conference on Christian Faith and Science in Society, Oxford, England, July 26-29, 1985.
Objective: Reviews advancements in the scientific study of spirituality and spiritual well-being. *Sample & Method*: Review and discussion. *Results & Conclusions*: Discusses developments in the definition of spirituality and attempts to include the spiritual dimension in health care. Examines research needs and reviews 8-10 instruments developed to assess spiritual well-being. Excellent references. *Quality*:

Good update (may write to Dr. Moberg at Marquette University, Milwaukee, Wisconsin 53233, for a copy).

287. Gorsuch, R.L. 1988. Psychology of religion. Annual Review of Psychology 39:201-221.
Objective: Review paper that examines the definitions of religion and spirituality, the operationalization of these definitions for research, and problems in measurement. *Sample and Methods*: Literature review and discussion. *Quality*: Excellent. Superb review by a renowned expert on the topic of measurement and religiosity. While not addressing the topic specifically in the elderly, this article will be useful for researchers as they devise specific instruments for assessing religiosity and spirituality in the aged.

288. Koenig, H.G. 1988. Construction and validation of the Springfield Religiosity Schedule [long and short versions]. In H. Koenig, M. Smiley, and J. P. Gonzales, Religion, Health, and Aging. Westport, CT: Greenwood Press, pp 171-187.
Objective: Develop a comprehensive, multi-dimensional, valid measure of religiousness in older adults. A long and short form of the SRS have been developed. *Sample & Methods*: The instrument includes an assessment of belief (Glock and Stark's (1966) "orthodoxy index"), of ritual (organizational and non-organizational), of experience (Glock and Stark 1966), of religious knowledge (Glock and Stark 1966), of the communal dimension (Lenski 1963), of spiritual well-being (religious well-being portion of Palouzian and Ellison's SWB index), and of intrinsic religiosity (Hoge 1972). Single items also tap religious coping and importance of prayer. *Results & Conclusions*: The SRS was validated in a sample of 85 ministers, priests, and rabbis located in the Springfield, Illinois area; strong agreement was the rule. Cronbach's alpha for different parts of the schedule were 0.61 for the organizational religious activity index, 0.63 for the nonorganizational religious activity index, and 0.87 for Hoge's intrinsic religiosity scale. Six-week test-retest reliability on 11 persons age 60 to 92 found an agreement of 92% for the 360 items of the SRS. The SRS is a valid and reliable instrument for measuring multiple dimensions of religiousness in an older population. Further information on scoring can be obtained from the author (Box 3400 Duke University Medical Center, Durham, NC 27710).

289. Kirschling, J.M., and J.F. Pittman. 1989. Measurement of spiritual well-being: A hospice caregiver sample. Hospice Journal 5(2):1-11.
Objective: Examines the reliability and validity of Paloutzian and

Ellison's Spiritual Well-Being (SWB) Scale in family caregivers of terminally ill patients. *Sample and Method*: Administered scale to 75 caregivers aged 27 to 84 (mean 62.3 years) of 70 terminally ill family members (aged 48-86 yrs); also measured caregiver affect using the Bradburn Affect Balance Scale. *Results*: High degree of internal consistency reliability was established (Cronbach's alpha 0.86 to 0.93). Construct validity, however, could not be established with the Bradburn Affect Scale. While spiritual well-being and positive affect were correlated in the expected direction, the association did not reach statistical significance; only the correlation between negative affect and existential well-being was significant. Religious well-being was not significantly related to either positive affect (r = +.15, p = ns) or negative affect (r = -.01, p = ns). *Conclusions*: The authors found little support for the validity of the SWB scale in this population of mainly older adults; spirituality may be too complex in later life to be captured entirely by this scale alone. *Quality*: Fair. The SWB Scale has been used in a large number of studies, but none to date in older adults; it combines "religious well-being" with "existential well-being"; the existential part of the scale, however, is heavily confounded by psychological items that would be expected to correlate strongly with mental health.

290.   Koenig, H.G.   1992.   The Religious Coping Index (RCI).
        Unpublished manuscript.   Duke University Medical Center,
        Durham, North Carolina 27710.

Objective: To develop a brief, non-offensive, acceptable, and easy to use observer-administered measure of religious coping to older medical patients. *Sample & Methods*: A 3-item measure of religious coping consisting of (1) an open-ended question about how the person copes, (2) a visual analogue scale from 0 to 10 upon which the person rates themselves on the degree to which they use religious beliefs or activities to help them to cope, and (3) based on a discussion of how religion helps them to cope and request for concrete examples of religious coping, the examiner rates the person from 0 to 10 on the degree to which they feel the patient uses religion to help them to cope. Thus, the index is composed of items involving spontaneous self report, self rating on a visual analogue scale, and an observer rating. *Results & Conclusions*: The scale score ranges from 0 to 30 and in an elderly medically ill population of 850 older men averaged 14.3 (S.D. 8.7). Inter-rater reliability in 188 consecutively hospitalized medically ill men was 0.81 (Pearson r); for the observer-rated item, reliability between two examiners with widely divergent religious orientations, was even higher (0.87) than for the overall index. For more information on the reliability and test characteristics of the RCI, see ref

52 [Koenig et al. 1992. <u>American Journal of Psychiatry</u> 149:1693-1700].

291. Williams, D.R. 1993. Measurement of religion. In J.S. Levin (Ed), <u>Religion in Aging and Health</u>, Thousand Oaks, CA: Sage, pp 125-148.
Objective: Reviews methods of conceptualizing and quantifying religious beliefs and behaviors that are relevant to older adults. *Sample & Methods*: Literature review & discussion. *Results & Conclusions*: Examines single and multidimensional measures of religion, examples of which are religious affiliation, church attendance, religious symbolism, subjective religiosity, intrinsic-extrinsic religion, and spiritual well-being.   Current studies are limited and deficient in their measurement of religion; the next generation of epidemiologic studies needs to include measures of religion that are conceptually based, validated, practical and cost-effective to administer. *Quality*: Good. *For other recent articles on the measurement of religion and spirituality see*: Bracki, M.A., J.M. Thibault, F.E. Netting, and J.W. Ellor.   1990. Principles of integrating spiritual assessment into counseling with older adults. <u>Generations</u> 14:55-58; Bufford, R.K., R.F. Paloutzian, and C.W. Ellison.   1991.   Norms for the Spiritual Well-being Scale.   <u>Journal of Psychology and Theology</u> 19:56-70 [research involving primarily younger subjects shows good reliability and validity as an overall assessment of spiritual well-being]; Thibault, J.M., J.W. Ellor, and F.W. Netting.   1991.   A conceptual framework for assessing the spiritual functioning and fulfillment of older adults in long-term care settings. <u>Journal of Religious Gerontology</u> 7:29-45. Ellor, J.W., and M.A. Bracki. 1995.   Assessment, referral and networking in pastoral care.   In M. Kimble, S.H. McFadden, J.W. Ellor, & J.J. Seeber (eds), <u>Aging, Religion, and Spirituality: A Handbook</u>. Minneapolis: Fortress Press.

Conclusions

The research literature has been expanding rapidly on the topic of religion and aging. Until 15 years ago, there had been relatively few systematic studies on this topic, particularly when compared to work done in other psychosocial domains such as social support, retirement, or economics. At present, virtually hundreds of papers have been published on religious practices in later life, changes in religiosity with age, religious faith development, religion's effects on mental and physical health, religion and ethical issues in later life, the role of the church and clergy in meeting the needs of older adults, networking between religious and social service agencies, the aging clergy, and the measurement of religiosity and spirituality. Unfortunately, these research reports have been scattered in dozens of professional journals in the fields of psychology, sociology, psychiatry, medicine, nursing, social work, education, gerontology, religion, and pastoral counseling. Even with advances in computer technology and library science, professionals in one field are frequently unexposed to parallel work being done in another field. For that reason, a volume such as Research on Religion and Aging was necessary.

What can we learn from the research that has been done over the past 15 years between 1980 and 1995? One thing is for certain. Religious behaviors and beliefs are extraordinarily common among the current generation of older adults living in the United States, and as far as we know, among older adults in other countries and cultures as well. These beliefs and practices have persisted for thousands of years, weathering advances in science, technology, and communication. Despite predictions by Freud and others that as society advanced religion would be replaced by the rational intellect, and that as people grew older and matured, they would "grow out" of the need for religion, this has simply not happened. According to

Gallup Polls, rates of church attendance in the United States in 1994 (40%) were virtually the same as in 1939, the year of Freud's death. If anything, people value their religious beliefs and practices more strongly as they grow older because of a greater need to use them in adapting to ill health, finding meaning in life, and confronting their own mortality.

Moreover, evidence from systematic research is accumulating in favor of a positive relationship between Judeo-Christian beliefs and practices and mental health in later life. Older adults themselves commonly report that religion is used to understand, cope with, and adapt to negative life events and health problems. In studies that have asked older adults open-ended questions about what enables them to cope with difficult life situations, between one-quarter and one-third will spontaneously give religious responses (God, prayer, faith, and so forth). Despite this well-documented tendency for older persons to turn to religion during times of physical illness or emotional turmoil, research has shown that the religious elderly have greater well-being, higher life satisfaction, less anxiety and depression, lower rates of suicide, less alcoholism, less loneliness, and adapt better to stress than do those elders without spiritual resources. Instead of religious coping behaviors breaking down during periods of high stress, they appear to have even greater utility during these times. Over and over again, studies are demonstrating that religion's positive effects on mental health are strongest among older persons who are disabled or under great stress from adverse life circumstances.

Thus, contrary to speculations by some mental health professionals that religion has mostly neurotic influences, Research on Religion and Aging documents the plethora of recent studies showing that Judeo-Christian religious behaviors (church attendance, Bible reading, prayer, etc.) and attitudes (intrinsic religiosity) in later life are associated with higher well-being, greater life satisfaction, and less depression. This is particularly true for older person with physical health problems and chronic disability, who at any given level of chronic medical illness are likely to view themselves as less disabled, and if disabled, were less likely to be depressed. Thus, religiousness may affect the way elders view their illness and the level of both physical and psychological dysfunction that it causes.

A major question that remains unanswered is how Judeo-Christian beliefs and activities convey their positive effects on mental health. Religious attitudes and behaviors may act in a number of ways to protect against the development of emotional problems in late life (Figure 1). Both the cognitive and the social aspects of religion are important in this process, and they are likely to act over the life-time of the individual. Religious background and upbringing, as well as the religious views and commitments of parents, can have an important impact on personality development. Religious prohibitions against smoking, drugs, alcohol, promiscuous sexual practices, and unhealthy dietary practices convey their effects on health over the lifetime of the individual, making them more or less vulnerable to physical illness in later life and to the psychological problems that follow. Perceptions of pain and disability are all affected by religious beliefs and practices that are crucial in conveying hope and maintaining motivation towards recovery. Because of the effects of religious belief on the older person's cognitive appraisal of stressful events, it can have a major moderating effect on the perception of the negative event. We have also seen in this section how religion affects the way older persons cope with stressful experiences like physical illness and loss. Religious coping behaviors may help avoid unhealthy behaviors like frank denial or a turning to alcohol or drug abuse as a way of handling the problem.

The social aspects of religion may be particularly important for many older adults in preventing loneliness, isolation, and depression, since the church is a major source of social support for elderly persons outside of their immediate family. In fact, older persons are more often involved in church groups than all other voluntary social groups combined. In a study of patients in a geriatric medicine clinic, we found that for 54% of patients, either four or five of their five closest friends came from their church congregations. The church is a readily available, acceptable, and inexpensive source of support for many older persons. Furthermore, the Judeo-Christian religious belief system encourages people to be concerned about and care for others. For this reason, it encourages altruistic activities that focus the elder's attention off of their own problems and onto the problems of others that are likely to be much worse than their own (downward social comparisons). Volunteer activities and the giving of oneself to help others, has been shown to enhance well-being and engender feelings of usefulness and purpose in older adults (Krause N. 1992. Providing support to others and well-being in later life. Journal of Gerontology 47:P300-P311).

Innovative and rapidly spreading programs are being developed by religious bodies to minister directly to the needs of older adults; particularly active in establishing such programs has been mainline denominations like the Methodist church, where 50% of members will be over age 60 by the year 2000. For example, the Methodist church has spear-headed the development of Shepherd's Centers. These programs, operated and managed entirely by older volunteers, seek to utilize the talents and abilities of healthy elders to provide services to sick or needy peers. These programs give older adults a feeling of purpose and self-esteem as they provide a valuable and needed

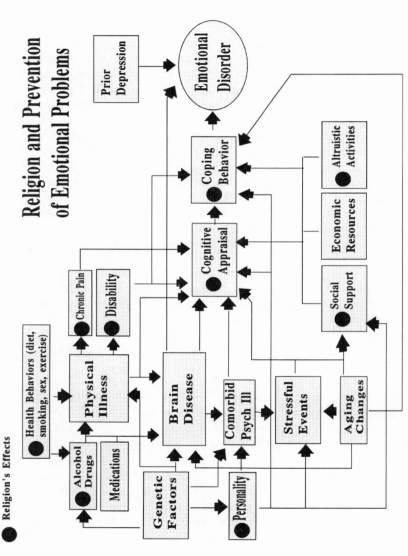

Figure 1. Hypothesized model of how religion may help prevent the development of emotional disorder in later life. Adapted from H. G. Koenig, D. G. Blazer, L. Hocking. 1995. Depression, anxiety and other affective disorders. In C. Cassel, H. J. Cohen, E. B. Larson, D. Meier, N. M. Resnick, L. Rubenstein, L. B. Sorensen (eds.), *Geriatric Medicine*, 3rd Edition, NY: Springer-Verlag.

services to their community. Services provided include respite care, education and health information, meals on wheels, transportation for medical visits, exercise and health maintenance. Shepherd's Centers are completely independent of state or federal influence, and are supported entirely by donations from local businesses and churches. The first Shepherd's Center was started in 1972 in Kansas City, Missouri. That program is now supported by over 25 churches and synagogues, and serves more than 6000 older adults through 400 elderly volunteers. Several articles in the Part III provide more information about these programs and their need. They are clearly a prototype for the future as churches become more and more burdened with the responsibility of taking care of the physical and emotional needs of older congregants.

Even if depression or anxiety problems develop in later life, religion may help facilitate their timely resolution (Figure 2). Much in the same way as that it prevents depression, it might speed recovery by influencing personality development (e.g., habitual ways of handling internal and external stressors), promoting drug or alcohol avoidance (which might exacerbate the problem), preventing earlier episodes of depression that might have made the current episode more treatment resistant, facilitating early recognition (by church members or the pastor), enhancing compliance with drug treatment or psychotherapy (religiosity enhances compliance), encouraging a healthy lifestyle, providing a social support group that cares and listens, and encouragement of altruistic activities that might distract the older person from their own problems. Again, by instilling hope, meaning, and purpose, religious beliefs could affect cognitive appraisal of events and provide alternative coping strategies.

Sociologists, gerontologists, nurses, medical physicians, and mental health professionals need to be aware of the effects that religion can have on older adults and the resource that it may represent. This is not to say that religion, when taken to its extreme and held rigidly and inflexibly, cannot cause both mental health problems and distress in relating with others. Nevertheless, the research over the past decade and a half has demonstrated that the positive effects of having a devout religious faith seem to outweigh its negative effects, particularly in later life.

What is the clinical relevance of these research findings? The clinical applications of knowledge about religion's effects on physical, mental, and social well-being of older adults have only recently been a topic of study. The research over the next decade will help define for professionals how spiritual resources can be utilized as tools to help prevent emotional distress, facilitate adaptation, and treat or manage mental disorders that arise in this age group. From a public health

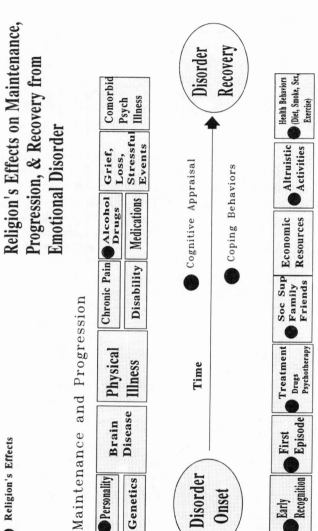

Religion's Effects on Maintenance, Progression, & Recovery from Emotional Disorder

● Religion's Effects

Maintenance and Progression

| Personality
Genetics | Brain
Disease | Physical
Illness | Chronic Pain
Disability | Alcohol
Drugs
Medications | Grief,
Loss,
Stressful
Events | Comorbid
Psych
Illness |

● Cognitive Appraisal

● Coping Behaviors

Time

Disorder Onset

| Early
Recognition | First
Episode | Treatment
Drugs
Psychotherapy | Soc Sup
Family
Friends | Economic
Resources | Altruistic
Activities | Health Behaviors
(Diet, Smoke, Sex,
Exercise) |

Recovery

Disorder Recovery

Emotional Disorder =
Depression & Anxiety

Figure 2. Hypothesized model of how religion may facilitate recovery from emotional disorder in later life.

perspective, it will be particularly important for health professionals to learn how to take advantage of a person's spiritual resources to help prevent or minimize disability from chronic illness. Ellen Idler is leading the field in this area at present.

It is not only health professionals, however, who need education about religion's effects on and importance to older persons. Recent Gallup Polls (1994 supplement to Religion in America, Princeton Religion Research Center, Princeton, NJ) provide data to indicate that by the year 2000, over 50% of mainline Protestants in the United States will be age 60 or over. The clergy also needs to be informed about the important role that they will increasingly play in providing physical, psychological, and social support to aging members over the next half-century, as 80 million baby boomers move into old age and triple the population of older adults in this country. Because of a rising federal deficit, expanding health care costs, and increasing numbers of older persons with chronic disability, dementia, depression, and other mental health problems, government resources will be increasingly scarce to meet the needs of older persons in America. Like always in history, the church will be called upon to act as a safety net to provide the physical and emotional needs of this age group when government programs fail. Whether the church will be willing or able to take on this necessary role remains to be seen.   The education of clergy on gerontological issues, including geriatric mental health problems, will be essential for their being able to carry out these tasks. Developing a working alliance between church, social service agencies, families, and healthy elderly living in the community, will be essential in a joint effort to meet the needs of frail elders of the future.

It is my hope that this annotated bibliography will help researchers, clinicians, and clergy to rapidly locate and evaluate the work that has already been done in the areas noted above. This will help prevent repetition, and advance the field forward based on the knowledge that has already accumulated.

Author Index

Subject Index

Adjustment to aging, 35-37; to childlessness, 35. See also Life satisfaction; Well-being
Age changes and religiosity, 5,14,15,19,37,40,83
Aging clergy, Catholic priests, 140-142; Catholic sisters, 43,44,140; Protestant clergy, 141
Alcohol use, 7,75-78,152; abstinence, 23,28; longevity, 102; pastoral counseling, 129; Pentecostals, 53; psychiatric patients, 75; religious beliefs and practices, 77,78; religious coping, 28; retirement community, 76; stress and abstinence, 77; Type A behavior, 92,93; well-being, 76
Allport, Gordon, 9,12,51,60,68
Anxiety, 51,152,155; baby boomers, xiii; Bible study/prayer, 48,49; "born again", 48,49; cancer, 66; chronic back pain, 62; chronic illness, 47; church

attendance, 48,49; denomination, 48,49; medical illness, 7; mental illness, 73; Muslims, 60; Pentecostals, 52; religious pilgrimage, 47,48; religious TV, 48,49; rural elderly, 36; women, 34. See also Death anxiety
Assisted-suicide, 122,124-126

Baby boomers, xiii,52,135,157
Beliefs of community elderly, 14; medical patients, 8; nurses, 8; old-old, 102; patients' families, 8; physicians, 8; well-being, 45
Beliefs (type), in afterlife, 14,40,73,75,125; Jewish, 6,85,125,146; Judeo-Christian, 7,12, 39,71,86-88,118,152
Bereavement, 50
Bible study, 15,20,48,49,53, 57,71,77,113,125,152
Blacks, 7,8,19-21,24,26-28, 47,51,53-59,61,62,71,72,

About the Compiler

HAROLD G. KOENIG, Assistant Professor of Psychiatry and Internal Medicine at Duke University Medical Center, is Director of the Program on Religion, Aging, and Health, one of the first academic and research programs of its kind in the United States. Dr. Koenig has received a five-year National Institutes of Mental Health Academic Award to study the diagnosis and treatment of depression in older persons with health problems. His recent books include *Religion, Health, and Aging* (Greenwood Press, 1988) and *Aging and God* (1994).

ISBN 0-313-29427-5

90000>

EAN

9 780313 294273

HARDCOVER BAR CODE